# Small Miracles II

Also by the authors:

*Small Miracles:*
Extraordinary Coincidences
from Everyday Life

# Small Miracles II

## Heartwarming Gifts of Extraordinary Coincidences

*Yitta Halberstam*
*&*
*Judith Leventhal*

ADAMS MEDIA CORPORATION
Holbrook, Massachusetts

For Motty —
*Who repairs the world every day
With a kind word, a warm smile, a generous act
Thus creating in his own unique way
Miracles.* — YHM

*Dedicated to the miracles in my life;
Jules, Arielle, and little Shira.
To my father of blessed memory, Harry B. Frankel.* — JFL

Published by
Adams Media Corporation
260 Center Street, Holbrook, MA 02343

ISBN: 1-58062-047-7

Printed in the United States of America.

First Edition
J I H G F E D C B A

**Library of Congress Cataloging-in-Publication Data**
Mandelbaum, Yitta Halberstam.
Small miracles II : heartwarming gifts of extraordinary coincidences /
Yitta Halberstam Mandelbaum & Judith Frankel Leventhal. — 1st ed.
p.    cm.
ISBN 1-58062-047-7 (pbk.)
1. Coincidence—Psychic aspects. I. Leventhal, Judith Frankel. II. Title.
BF1175.M363        1998
133.8—dc21        98-23946
CIP

Cover art by Barry David Marcus.

*This book is available at quantity discounts for bulk purchases.
For information, call 1-800-872-5627 (in Massachusetts, 781-767-8100).*

Visit our home page at http://www.adamsmedia.com

# *Introduction*

Throughout our journey in life we encounter many teachers and signposts that lead us along our way. They whisper words of wisdom and encouragement to us as we struggle and yearn; they invite us into new spheres of Being and Existence. They let us know that in our existential loneliness we are not alone—that Spirit surrounds us always.

Chief among these signposts and teachers is none other than the phenomenon that some choose to call coincidence, but that we—the authors—recognize and firmly believe are nothing more and nothing less than "small miracles."

And it is precisely at this moment in time that we need "small miracles" in our lives—now more than ever before.

Why is the identification of coincidences as "small miracles" crucial to our spiritual and personal growth?

When a person dismissively shrugs off a "coincidence" as merely a random event or pure happenstance, he is doing himself—and the universe—a grave disservice. He is failing to apprehend a divine moment that was gifted to him by God, a ripe and full moment that comes in the great flow of energy in which he is a spark. Had he recognized the coincidence for what it truly is—God's gentle tap on the shoulder or

God's veritable shout: "Hello from Heaven!"—his spark would have united with other scattered sparks and ignited into one giant flame. He would have entered a corridor into a different dimension, and his days and nights would have been illuminated by a brilliant light. But the opportunity for endless transformation is lost when "coincidences" are perceived in pedestrian terms as simply "luck" or "chance."

How much more fortunate is the individual possessing enough awareness to recognize coincidences for what they truly are—mysterious, magical, and awe-inspiring testimonials to God's presence in our ordinary, everyday lives. This graced individual will most assuredly be filled with what we like to call "spiritual optimism." She will believe that the events in her life have purpose, that the "coincidences" in her life have purpose and that—most important of all—her very life is hallowed by sacred purpose. She will see the holiness of day-to-day existence, the holiness of herself. And, in a world where nihilistic forces threaten at times to submerge us, this is the greatest blessing of all.

To believe that nothing is an accident, but that everything is foreordained, fills us, paradoxically, with both vigor and serenity. It makes us examine our lives more closely; makes us more attentive to detail. And, as the saying goes: "God is in the details." Cultivating consciousness about the "coincidences" that come into our lives fills us with excitement and gratitude. We feel that we are truly God's children and that He is with us, always.

During our book tour for *Small Miracles* last year, we were continuously made aware of the amazing role that the power of belief plays in choreographing the flow of our lives. We saw with tremendous clarity the workings of the spiritual principle that *thoughts create realities,* and that *vibrating a certain energy attracts a like energy to it.* What do we mean by this?

When you believe in coincidences, they pour into your life at an exhilarating, almost dizzying rate. When you require something from the universe, and you truly believe that the universe is responsive, then you most assuredly will receive its full bounty for the asking.

Here are just a few examples that vividly illustrate this point:

On book tour, we lived, breathed, dreamed, ate, and spoke "coincidences." Our consciousness was clearly in alignment with the universe's. As a result, strange things happened almost every day.

We had talked incessantly about approaching one of the most famous spiritual writers of our time to discuss *Small Miracles.* Since we were not personally acquainted with him, we faced a challenge. How to meet the man and humbly submit our request? We explored many avenues, and finally it was decided that Yitta would enroll in a one-night course that the "guru" was giving. Surely at some time during the three-hour class there would be a window of opportunity that Yitta could seize to our advantage. However, a day before the course was scheduled, we were disappointed to learn that it had been canceled due to the teacher's unexpected illness. Now what? It was a setback, but we were not discouraged. We both vibrated an intense need to meet this man. The very next week Judith flew to Washington, D.C., on book tour, sat in the airplane seat that had been "randomly" assigned to her, and discovered . . . to her shock and delirious joy . . . that her seatmate was none other than the spiritual guru we had resolved to meet! Not only did they engage in animated discussion during the entire plane ride, but after swapping personal biographies they discovered that they had lived in the exact same house in Crown Heights, Brooklyn, when Judith was a toddler and the spiritual leader was a college student, and that the spiritual leader's parents had been Judith's parents' landlords many years ago!

During Yitta's book tour to Brookline, Massachusetts, she wandered early one spring morning through the maze of leafy residential streets in search of a restaurant where she could have breakfast. Finding herself hopelessly lost, she approached the first person she saw walking down the street and asked for directions. She explained that she was from New York and didn't know her way around the neighborhood. The man smiled pleasantly and said that he too was originally from New York, and asked her name. When she introduced herself, the man's smile froze, and he took a few steps back and stared at her in incredulity. Then he recovered his composure and introduced himself. "I am Yitzhak Halberstam," he said simply, "your long-lost cousin!"

One of our favorite stories in the first *Small Miracles* book came from the *Oprah Winfrey Show*'s Valentine's Day special of 1996, which featured an elderly couple who had been married for over fifty years. We wrote the story based on the transcript of the show, but were unable to track down the individuals themselves, a fact we greatly lamented. We often spoke of our great desire to meet them personally, but they had asked Oprah's producers for privacy, and their whereabouts were shrouded in secrecy. We had no idea where they lived. One evening, Judith was delivering a talk at the Barnes and Noble bookstore in Bayside, Queens, and during the question and answer period that followed, a hand shot up from someone sitting in the back. "Page 129," he announced proudly. "Ex-excuse me?" Judith stammered, confused. "You wrote our story on page 129 of your book," the man repeated genially. It was the Valentine's Day couple from the *Oprah Winfrey Show* — the couple we had yearned to meet for so long!

During another question and answer period — this one following a talk we gave to eight hundred people in Baltimore — a woman stood up and announced her validation of the perspective on coincidences that we had just offered. "Whenever I need something," she stated confidently, "I just talk to God and tell him what it is I require, and then he gives it to me." She went on to say that she constantly won door prizes at parties—and she always won items that she had a specific need for. After this woman spoke, the question and answer period was wrapped up, and the second part of the program—a raffle—was begun. When the Grand Prize raffle winner—chosen randomly onstage by a blindfolded Yitta, who plunged her hand into a box containing hundreds of tickets—was announced, a collective gasp was heard throughout the auditorium. Guess who the winner was???

When we pray, we are speaking to God. When "coincidences" occur, it is God speaking to us. To be attuned to these moments is truly to be awake to the Divine that calls us every day.

But beyond providing us with testimonials to God's presence in a spiritually barren landscape where there are few useful clues, "coincidences" also contain within themselves precious moral lessons and profound teachings. Many of the stories in this book revolve around the concept of what some people call "karma," a certain payback the protagonist receives from the universe, a manifestation that "what goes around comes around." Other stories illustrate how the universe answers—through a seeming coincidence—a question or prayer the protagonist has articulated; still other stories demonstrate the age-old wisdom that we always reap the harvest of seeds that we sow in life.

When "coincidences" happen and we are aware of the messages we are being sent, a delicious sense of communion, of harmony with the universe, unfolds. We sense that everything is One, and that if we can only integrate these messages—these little bulletins from God—we can grow as moral and spiritual beings.

We are exhilarated when coincidences come into our lives, for we see them as blessings and gifts. Many people bemoan the lack of open, revealed miracles in the late twentieth century, maintaining that their absence makes the sustenance of faith that much harder. Seas don't part; God doesn't appear in a pillar of flame to talk with us; recalcitrant humans are not transmogrified into columns of salt. And it *is* true—the more grandiose, apocalyptic miracles of yesteryear do seem elusive. Nonetheless, we staunchly maintain that "small miracles" are everywhere, and that awareness of their existence can lead us to renewed faith.

Many people have written and told us that after they read *Small Miracles*, momentous changes began to occur in their lives, and that as soon as they opened their hearts to "coincidences," the coincidences came flowing in. Or they began to examine the past with a different eye and recognized that miracles had been happening all along, but they simply hadn't identified them by their rightful name! We hope that a newfound awareness will develop in your life after reading this book, and that you, too, will begin experiencing the wonders, the bounty, the splendors of life that resonate with those who believe in "small miracles."

"There are only two positions you can take," Albert Einstein once said. "Either you believe that nothing in life is a miracle, or you believe that *everything* in life is a miracle."

It is clear that the individual whose journey in life is more joyous, more meaningful, and more sublime, is the individual who subscribes to the second view.

By opening the pages of this book, you have already begun the voyage.

Travel with us into the Light, as we bless and receive the joy that "small miracles" always bring.

---

*Note:* Names followed by an asterisk are pseudonyms.

*She* wanted to live out in the country, where the poet in her could find its muse, and be inspired.

I was a hard-nosed reporter whose pulse quickened at the sound of a police siren or the wail of an ambulance — who liked the fast tempo of city life, the energy it sizzled with, the babble of different tongues, the gritty noise of survival. Besides, I was a rising young star in the world of broadcast news, and I couldn't give up my job now at the big station where I worked. There was nothing for me out there in the country, and a long commute to the city was unappealing.

As always, she was the one asked to make the sacrifices in our marriage, the one who deferred a dream.

"At least," she sighed with resignation, "a big yard with lots of trees and bushes and flowers and birds."

I promised her that and I kept my word.

The house was small but it came with a wraparound deck that overlooked magnificent and sprawling grounds. There was a large expanse of lush grass dotted by majestic trees, evergreen bushes, a rose garden, even a vegetable patch.

"Perfect!" she breathed. "It's a little oasis where I can retreat. Where *we* can retreat," she corrected herself, stealing a sidelong glance at me.

"Promise me you'll sit out here with me every now and then and just inhale the beauty of the scene," she begged.

I laughed. I had married a nineties hippie, into meditation and alternative health, whose soul was stirred by a verdant expanse of rolling lawn. We were so different—but she brought a kind of music into my life that I had never quite heard before.

I kept that promise, too. Every now and then, I would join her on the deck and, despite myself, be moved by the idyllic scene. Sometimes we moved our chairs together from the deck into the yard itself, where branches from the old oak trees were entwined and formed a canopy over our heads.

It was a month after we had moved into the house that we first saw them. A pair of cardinal birds, hidden in one of the evergreen bushes, suddenly alighted onto the ground—a dash of vivid and warm color only a few yards from where we sat.

"Look!" she exclaimed, with the delight of a young child. "It's husband and wife!"

"Cardinals get married?" I teased.

"They mate for life," she said.

"I didn't know that," I answered.

"You never, ever see a female cardinal without a male. And what's nice is he always defers to her. He always lets her feed first. I really find that very sweet."

"But how can you tell which is the male and which is the female?" I asked, confused.

"Oh," she laughed, "you don't know anything about birds at all, do you? There is no bird more easily recognizable than the male cardinal, almost entirely red except for the conspicuous black mask on his face. And see? The female cardinal's overall color is buff-brown and yellowish-olive."

"You never cease to amaze me with all the stuff you know," I said.

"Wait till you hear them sing!" she enthused. "They are proud musicians. Their notes are very distinctive and beautiful, kinda like the quality of a small bell being rung. They sing different songs, too. The song they sing in the winter sounds something like "pretty, pretty, pretty," but their spring ballad is more piercing and poignant: a series of sounds that sort of descend into a kinda 'sweet slurring' and that some people describe as 'cheer, cheer' or 'dear, dear.'"

"When they look at you," I said lovingly, "they're clearly singing 'pretty, pretty.'"

"Oh, you!" she giggled, planting a tender kiss on my cheek.

For months the cardinals came, visiting us on a regular basis. She knew that they loved sunflower seeds, and she kept a huge bag stored in the pantry. As faithful as they were to each other, they became equally devoted to us. Every day they became more and more emboldened, until they were only a few feet away. They always sat opposite us—like mirror images—the female opposite my wife, the male opposite me. They watched us carefully, and we watched them, and my wife fancied that the pair of cardinals were metaphors for life, or at the very least, for *our life.* We felt we were all connected in some great cosmic way. Even I, the entrenched cynic, was beginning to feel some bond that was bigger than all of us combined.

And then something strange and mysterious and anomalous began to happen—something that, according to my wife the expert, definitely deviated from patterns of typical cardinal behavior.

Whenever my wife would sit out alone in the yard, only the female cardinal would come to visit. And when I had occasion to unwind in the garden and sat by myself in the lounge chair, only the male cardinal would make an appearance. But when we both sat outside together, the cardinals would come to call as a pair, and would sit opposite us side by side, as they always did. It was as if the two birds were beginning to mirror our lives more and more.

And then the day came when we sat outside together no more.

It was galloping leukemia, the doctors said, and it took her very fast. Six weeks after the diagnosis, she was gone.

At first, I couldn't venture into the yard at all. It held too many memories of our best times together, the times when I held her close and she melted my heart. But then I wanted to be in the place where her memory was the strongest—and it was there in the yard, surrounded by the nature that touched her spirit so.

So I hazarded a few steps into the garden, looked around at the lush foliage that had entranced her soul, and sat down in the lounge chair that remained where it had been left. I leaned back in the chair and covered my face with my hands, and the tears began to fall.

It was then that I heard it . . . a beautiful vocalization, a full-fledged song. I raised my eyes and saw the male cardinal . . . alone . . . sitting opposite me, a few feet away. I fancied that he looked mournful and had come to pay a condolence call.

The female cardinal was nowhere to be seen.

And just as my wife had once told me, the song in the spring *was* different from the one in the winter. In the winter, it was just one note, but now it was a series of sounds that descended into a sweet slurring.

And I could swear on my life that what I clearly heard that day was the cardinal's commiseration, a vocalization that sounded like "cheer, cheer" or "dear, dear."

Now I always retreat to the chair in the yard, which has become both my sanctuary and my mourning stool, and the male cardinal faithfully returns to keep me company, day after day, alone.

—*Steven Richards*

### Comment
There is a melody that pulsates through the universe, and its song is that we are all one.

$A$*ll* his life, Andy Golembiewski was known as both a mischievous prankster and a warmhearted Good Samaritan. As owner of Andy's Bar and Grill, a tavern in Lawrenceville, he was a neighborhood fixture with a reputation for playing pranks on his customers but also lending them money when they were short. He believed that helping another human being in time of need was the greatest good a man could do. He provided well for his family members in life—and they believe he worked in mysterious ways to provide well for them in death too.

At the age of eighty-three, Andy contracted prostate cancer, and in the summer of 1997 his condition took a noticeable turn for the worse. One night in August, he fell into a coma, and his grieving family gathered at his bedside, braced for the inevitable. When hope for an improvement in Andy's condition had all but vanished and he had been unconscious for hours, his eyelids suddenly fluttered. His fingers began to quiver, and his body trembled. Then his eyes flew open, and they darted around the room with a gleam of intelligence and lucidity. He propped himself on his arms, looked his granddaughter Debra White in the eye, and said loudly and clearly, "1 . . . 6 . . . 9 . . . 5." And then as suddenly as he had stirred, he fell back onto the bed unconscious, and a few hours later he died.

His relatives didn't know what to make of it. They all agreed that Andy had appeared perfectly rational and clearheaded when he had uttered the four numbers. But what did these numbers mean? They had clung to the hope that he would awaken from the coma to bask in their love and receive a last embrace. In turn, they had yearned for some final words of love from Andy, or some crowning and climactic nugget of wisdom that would cap his life and serve as a departing testament. But . . . numbers? What kind of message from the grave was that?

"Those were the very last words he uttered," said his daughter-in-law, Millie Golembiewski. "Nobody could figure out the significance of this number. It wasn't anybody's birthday, phone number, address. Nothing connected."

For the next several hours, the relatives puzzled. They could not shake their conviction that Andy's words held import, and they tried to make sense of his communication. What could those numbers mean?

It was Andy's son, Tony, who finally suggested that they play the Big Four Lottery, which was being held the next day.

The next evening they were celebrating a very bizarre and bittersweet lottery win of $23,500.

"Andy!" his widow screamed, as the numbers were called up. "You're so concerned about your family, you even paid for your own funeral!"

The win was ironic, his family told reporters later, because during his lifetime Andy was opposed to gambling and had never even once played the lottery.

"He was a prankster," said his granddaughter. "I think he's up there laughing that we only put a dollar on the number."

"He was so kindhearted," another relative told a TV crew, "that he had to look out for his family even after he was gone."

*O*ne hot summer day, a young couple and their four-year-old daughter, Tzippie, were on their way to the mountains for a few weeks' vacation. Suddenly, a huge truck in the oncoming lane collided head-on with the family's small car. The couple was injured seriously, and little Tzippie sustained many fractures. They were immediately taken to the nearest hospital, where Tzippie was brought to the children's ward and her parents were taken to the intensive care unit. As can well be imagined, Tzippie was not only in great pain, but she was also very frightened because her parents were not nearby to give her comfort.

Martha, the nurse who was assigned to Tzippie, was a single, older woman. She understood Tzippie's fear and insecurity and became very devoted to her. When Martha finished her shift, instead of going home, she would volunteer to stay with Tzippie at night. Of course, Tzippie grew very fond of her and depended on her for her every need. Martha brought her cookies, picture books, and toys; she sang songs to her and told her countless stories.

When Tzippie was able to be moved, Martha put her in a wheelchair and took her to visit her parents every day. After many months of hospitalization, the family was discharged. Before they left the hospital, the parents blessed Martha for her devoted and loving care and invited her to visit them. Tzippie would not let go of

Martha, and insisted that she come to live with them. Martha also did not want to be parted from her little Tzippie, but her life was in the children's ward of the hospital, and she could not think of leaving. There was a tearful parting as Tzippie and the loving nurse said good-bye to each other. For a few months the family kept up a close relationship with Martha—through phone calls only, since they lived quite a distance from her. When they moved abroad, however, they lost contact with each other.

Over thirty years passed. One winter Martha, who was now in her seventies, became seriously ill with pneumonia and was hospitalized in the geriatric ward of a hospital near her home. There was a certain nurse on duty who noticed that Martha had very few visitors. She tried her best to give the elderly lady special care, and she saw that she was a sensitive, clever person.

One night when the nurse was sitting near her elderly patient and they were chatting quietly, she confided in her as to what had prompted her to become a nurse. When she was four years old, she explained, and her parents had been injured in an automobile accident, there had been a wonderful nurse who had brought her back to health with her loving, caring devotion. As she grew older, she determined that one day she, too, would become a nurse and help others—from the young to the old—just as that nurse had done for her.

After she graduated from nursing school overseas, she had met a young man from America, and when they married, they moved to the States. A few months ago they had moved to this city, where her husband had been offered a very good job, and she was happy to get a position as a nurse in this hospital. As the nurse's story unfolded, tears flowed from the elderly patient's eyes, as she realized that this must surely be her little Tzippie, whom she had cared for after the accident.

When the nurse had finished her story, Martha said softly, "Tzippie, we are together again, but this time *you* are nursing *me!*" Tzippie's eyes opened wide as she stared at Martha, suddenly recognizing her. "Is it really you?" she cried out. "How many times I have thought about you and prayed that someday we would meet again!"

When Martha recovered from her illness, Tzippie— this time—did not beg her to come and live with her family. Instead, she just packed up Martha's belongings and took her home with her. She lives with Tzippie to this day, and Tzippie's husband and children have welcomed her like a most special grandmother.

—*Ruchoma Shain*

### Comment

In the circle of love, we are all givers and receivers. First we are one, then we are the other . . . the circle keeps turning around and around.

*W*e live in a rural town in Montana—small enough for everyone to know his neighbors. At best the census taker might clock us all in at one thousand residents. The winters here are cold and deep. When some friends in Southern California invited us to visit them, my brother Steve and I decided to take that "once-in-a-lifetime" trip. For a week we could enjoy the warm climate and just relax with our wives and four children during the Christmas break. The kids were especially excited about visiting Disneyland.

We started planning the trip two months in advance. It made economic sense, we felt, to travel together in a recreational vehicle that was large and comfortable enough to accommodate us all. Our mother, a first grade school teacher, was also on her Christmas break and asked if she could join us. In fact, she insisted. This struck me as odd, since my father showed no interest in our plans and, understandably, preferred to stay home. No lengthy journeys in a crowded van for him. But I saw the gleam in her eye, and of course, we had to say, "Yes, come along."

We drove for two days before reaching our friends' home south of Los Angeles. The following day we were all basking in the sun at Disneyland. It surpassed our children's wildest dreams. The next two days we visited other tourist spots in the area.

For the final day of the vacation, the family voted to make a return trip to Disneyland. I, however, had a quite different idea—at least for myself. I told my family that I wanted to venture out on my own to see Los Angeles. I would get there on the city bus and see the sights—a stunning contrast, I knew, to our small home town.

My host was most helpful the evening before. Together we made a plan so that I could make the most of my few hours in Los Angeles and—importantly—my host gave me a map of downtown to keep me from getting lost. I went to bed excited about my upcoming adventure.

The next morning when my host was about to drive me to the bus stop, I saw my mother running toward the car. She had originally planned to go with the others, but now, suddenly, she wanted to spend the day with me. I said: "Mother, that's not a good idea. More than likely we'll get lost and accidentally end up in some rough part of town." We continued to argue, but she would have none of it. There was no changing her mind. I had to concede, and she jumped into the car.

The first part of the bus trip into the city was very pleasant. Mother and I had a lively conversation about family and friends. Proceeding to the "inner city," the bus made stops about every two blocks to let passengers on and off—passengers of every conceivable nationality, color, and income level. Suddenly, mother and I were a minority of two. This didn't bother us. Our hosts assured us we would be perfectly safe.

However, as we approached a rundown part of town I became apprehensive. Although it was the middle of the day, I sensed that I had made a big mistake taking my mother into this area. When we reached the last stop the bus driver noticed our concern. "You'll be all right," he said. "You're only five minutes from downtown. Any of the drivers can give you additional directions."

Stepping off the bus, we were surrounded by old, dilapidated buildings. Street people were all around us. We were rather scared. Before approaching anyone for directions to another bus, we thought we might find some spot to rest and let our blood pressures settle down. We stuck closely together and started around the block in search of a store or restaurant that might possibly have a restroom. We had no desire to spend any time or money in the area. Canvassing both sides of the block we found a store that suited our temporary needs. We kept watch for one another while we used the restrooms.

Upon leaving the store we turned to the right and—quite suddenly—we came face to face with the shock of our lives. Before us was a homeless man. His hair was long and dirty. His beard nearly reached his belt. His stained clothes hung loosely on his thin frame. I couldn't look at him. But I had to. He was my brother, Doug. He was my mother's first child. Gone was the star high school athlete. Gone was the college graduate. Gone was the Vietnam veteran. He had never recovered from that terrible experience. He was now a schizophrenic. His only words to us were: "Hi, what are you guys doing here?"

There was really nothing to say. My mother embraced him. She brushed the hair from his face. I brushed the tears from my eyes. Two years ago Doug had boarded a Greyhound bus on a warm summer day without telling any of us. His destination was Los Angeles—a city of 13 million. He rented an apartment for a couple of months until his money ran out. Since then, he had been living on the street, begging for food, and sleeping in doorways under cardboard blankets.

This unexpected encounter was our first contact with him in two years. Now I realized why my mother had to come with me on the bus that day. She had a mission, and she completed it.

When my mother and I left Doug in the middle of that sad street, we both felt, understandably, that we would never see Doug again. Happily that did not prove to be the case. Doug, on his own, returned a few months later to Montana, where I helped him get situated at the Rescue Mission in my town. For the last ten years I have met him every Sunday afternoon for coffee and pie at the mission, where he now is able to work a few hours each day in the mission's thrift shop. He tells me about his personal discoveries as he walks endlessly around town. In short, he has come to have a life of his own that he considers satisfying and useful.

Although they live some two hours away, Mom and Dad visit Doug every other month or so. About twice a year he boards a bus—not to drop out of sight as he originally had done—but to go back home again and spend a few days with them. Because Doug is at peace with himself and his special world, I now realize that this never would have happened but for the fact that on one cold December day my mother and I boarded that fateful bus to Los Angeles.

—*Dave DeBoer*

❧

### Comment

The universe provides its own system of transportation to carry us to the places we most need to be.

*In* 1919, my grandfather Aaron Lazer was a struggling young scholar, newly married, with a pregnant wife and no viable means of support. He worked part-time at his mother's shop in the town of Koscive, Czechoslovakia, but the wages he brought home were meager, and the store's earnings were not adequate to sustain two families. Regretfully, his mother advised him that it was time for him to strike out on his own, and Aaron took her counsel to heart.

Indeed, Aaron *wanted* to be on his own—self-sufficient and independent—and he felt he possessed both the initiative and the savvy to become a successful businessman. So he began to cast about for something to do that would launch his career.

World War I had just ended, and Czechoslovakia was experiencing many serious shortages, both in food supply and in other sectors. The leather goods industry was particularly hard hit, and good, sturdy shoes were difficult to come by. At that time, most shoes were of necessity being fashioned from cardboard and paper, and they did not hold up well. My grandfather decided that this was the opportune time to open up a shoe business that would fill an important vacuum and offer strong, solid footwear.

Aaron borrowed 5,000 kronin—a princely sum in those days—and traveled to a large city to seek out an agent who brokered shoes. He returned home after several days weary but elated. His mission had been accomplished. In the back of his wagon were several cartons of heavy military shoes. He had used all his money to buy five hundred pairs—a risk, to be sure—but he was convinced they would be eagerly snapped up by the local townspeople and that he would make a veritable killing. Imagine Aaron's despair when he opened the cartons to proudly display the merchandise to his family, and found that instead of five hundred pairs, he owned a thousand right-foot shoes only!

Heart-rending sobs tore from him as he stared in shock at the row of right shoes lined up in a long, mocking procession. Not a single left shoe among them!

His merchandise was utterly worthless, and he now owed huge sums of money to relatives, neighbors, and friends who had lent him, at great personal sacrifice, the kronin they had frugally hoarded for years.

How was he ever going to recoup his losses? How was he ever going to repay his loans? How was he going to support his wife and new baby? How was he going to save face in a town that had placed its collective trust in him? No, no, it was too much to bear, and the almost inhuman, unearthly wails that Aaron emitted testified to his anguish.

Everyone urged him to return immediately to the big city, find the unscrupulous broker from whom he had bought the merchandise, and demand a refund. But when Aaron backtracked to the marketplace where he had originally encountered the man, he found that he had vanished. No one seemed to know anything about him—who he was, where he lived, where else he did business. All leads to him ran cold. It was as if he had never existed. Aaron wondered whether he had hallucinated the whole deal. But no, the nightmare was real enough: he had a thousand right shoes in his wagon, and all his money was gone.

He returned home despondent and inconsolable. His wife looked with concern at his pale, wan face and urged him to visit the wisest person they knew, a holy man who lived in Koscive and was renowned for his gentle wisdom and spiritual greatness. "Don't give up!" she exhorted her husband. "This man has helped many people. Maybe he can help you too."

Aaron tried to put on a brave front as he was ushered into the wise man's office, but as he stepped across the threshold, he burst into a torrent of tears. As he described the terrible fraud that had been perpetrated upon him, the great sage's face became suffused with sympathy for Aaron's downcast spirit. His words were sincere and kind.

"This is what you must do," the holy man murmured softly. "Go and pray, recite psalms and God will help. Have faith. All will be well."

Dutifully, Aaron followed the wise man's advice and sequestered himself in prayer in the synagogue. For several days, he wept and prayed, prayed and wept, focused only on his torment, unable to distill other forms of reality. Rivulets of tears flowed down his face and wet his cheeks. He had surrendered completely to his pain and was oblivious to his immediate surroundings. Aaron was so consumed by his misery that he was completely unaware that sympathetic congregants were tiptoeing softly around his sobbing figure, or that his compassionate wife was bringing him hot plates of steaming food, which he ate heedlessly. He had become so preoccupied, in fact, by the obsessive thoughts of failure and ruin that tortured him that he failed to observe a stranger quietly enter, retreat to a reclusive corner, and begin to sob himself. But when the man's heart-rending cries had escalated to ghastly shrieks, even Aaron's armorlike oblivion was pierced.

The man's cries tore at him and woke him from his days-long stupor. He didn't know the man, but he recognized the timbre of the cry. The man was in great emotional pain, that much was clear. Laboriously Aaron rose from his seat and crossed the room to approach him. He didn't know whether or not at this point he possessed the emotional resources to help the man, but he was the only one in the synagogue and the man clearly needed help.

As Aaron approached, he noticed a Book of Psalms on the stranger's lap, from which he was reciting in between sobs.

"Welcome," Aaron said, extending his hand. "I heard you crying and my heart goes out to you in your pain. Is there anything I can do to help?"

The stranger shook his head mournfully. "No one can help," he cried out in dejection. "I borrowed a lot of money to buy merchandise for a business. Alas, it was my terrible misfortune to be cheated by a dishonest merchant. I thought I was buying five hundred pairs of military shoes, but it turned out that the carton contained no pairs at all, but only a thousand shoes for the *left foot!*"

The stranger with the red-rimmed eyes looked sadly into my grandfather's red-rimmed eyes and was bewildered by the happy gleam that suddenly began to dance in them.

"My dear friend," my grandfather said as he draped a consoling arm around his soon-to-be partner, "I have very good news for you."

My grandfather and the stranger paired up the shoes (they were perfectly matched), sold them, and made a tremendous amount of money. Consequently, my grandfather became a very rich man, and this incident secured his position, both in the financial world of Czechoslovakia and in the annals of our family yore.

—*Chayke Lobl*

*Comment*
In any enterprise, God is the silent partner.

*R*ichard Fleming*, a retired businessman, was doing paperwork at home one Monday afternoon when the phone rang.

"Mr. Fleming?" a cool, crisp voice said. "This is Lauren from Dr. Brown's office. I just wanted to confirm your appointment with the doctor tomorrow morning at nine o'clock."

"An appointment with Dr. Brown?" Mr. Fleming repeated slowly, dully. He knitted his brows in puzzlement and turned to his wife with a perplexed look.

"What's the matter?" she whispered urgently, moving quickly to his side.

"Did I make an appointment with Dr. Brown that I totally forgot about?" he asked her, befuddled.

He had been to see Dr. Brown, a renowned Manhattan cardiologist, half a year before, and had been given a clean bill of health. He had no recollection of being advised to come in for another checkup in six months, nor did he recall making such an appointment.

"Can you just hang on for a minute, please?" he asked the doctor's secretary, while he hunted for his calendar. He was usually so careful about recording all his engagements, but the doctor's appointment wasn't penciled in.

---

* A pseudonym.

"Oh, no!" he mouthed to his wife. "Am I beginning to suffer from Alzheimer's?"

"Are you sure about the appointment?" he asked the nurse, returning to the phone.

"This *is* Richard Fleming?" she asked, more brusquely this time.

"Yes, of course it is."

"Well, Mr. Fleming, I have you down for a nine o'clock."

"Lauren," he confessed, "I don't remember making this appointment."

"Listen, Mr. Fleming," she snapped, all traces of civility now gone. "Dr. Brown is one of the busiest and most important cardiologists in New York. Appointments with him have to be booked months in advance. I have a long list of people waiting for a cancellation. If you don't want to come in, just tell me, and I'll call one of them. But you have to tell me right now whether you're coming or not, because this is a very busy office, and I don't have all day!"

"What should I do?" Richard mouthed to his wife.

"Go!" she shrugged. "If you made an appointment, it's not nice for you to cancel at the last minute."

"OK," he told Lauren, "I'm coming; I'll be there tomorrow morning."

"Fine," she breathed, sounding friendlier and less hostile. "See you tomorrow morning, then. You'll get the usual battery of tests. Just take it easy today and relax."

But Richard Fleming was unable to heed the secretary's counsel. All day long, he fretted over his apparent slip-up. A close friend had recently begun to experience serious memory loss and had been diagnosed with possible early Alzheimer's. Of all the terrors he associated with advancing age, Richard Fleming was most afraid of losing his mind. Was his inability to remember the appointment an impending and ominous sign?

The next morning, he underwent a grueling series of tests in Dr. Brown's office. "When they're all over," he kept vowing to himself, "I'm going to bring up the subject of Alzheimer's."

But he didn't have the opportunity, because after Dr. Brown had begun to evaluate the results, he returned to Mr. Fleming's room, a grim expression on his face.

"Not a moment too soon!" he exclaimed. "You're a lucky man, Mr. Brown. You have a serious cardiac problem, and you'll have to go in for surgery immediately. It's fortunate that you had an appointment today," the doctor added. "Had this problem not been detected soon, you would surely have been in serious trouble within a month or two."

Meanwhile, at the secretary's desk in the reception room, an irate man was causing a minor commotion.

"What do you mean, Richard Fleming is already in the doctor's office? *I am* Richard Fleming!"

One young nurse rolled her eyes meaningfully at the secretary, as if to say: "What some brazen people won't do these days to get an appointment." But the older secretary's eyes clouded with consternation, and her face grew pale when the man withdrew an official appointment card that had been issued to him from the doctor's office.

"Here!" he shouted, shoving the appointment card under her nose. "See for yourself. It's today's date, and it says nine o'clock." He started flinging various forms of identification from his wallet. "And here is my driver's license and several credit cards, which I assume," he screamed, "will prove that I am none other than Richard Fleming!"

"Then who," the young nurse asked, bewildered, "is the man sitting in the doctor's office right now?"

"Wait a second," said the secretary slowly, "let me check my records." And there she found two separate files for two different Richard Flemings—one who lived in Manhattan and was currently fuming in the reception room, another who lived in Brooklyn and was currently being given a serious diagnosis together with the prescription for cure.

The wrong Richard Fleming had been called by the secretary.

Only it was really the *right* Richard Fleming—the one who needed the coincidence to happen in order for his life to be saved!

❦

*Comment*

An event can be seen as a mistake or a miracle depending on the prism through which you view your life.

*N*othing is purer than the joy in a child's smile. Nothing elicits that smile more than love . . . and sometimes, the perfect present. That is what Louisa knew as the days approached until her daughter Stephanie's tenth birthday.

What she would give to make her precious daughter smile! For each day was a challenge to little Stephanie, who had been born deaf. She lived in a virtually silent world. Not an echo, not a buzz, not a sound. Louisa was trying her best to raise her daughter with love and instill a feeling of self-confidence in her. She provided Stephanie with everything she possibly could.

So of course, the child's tenth birthday should be something special. And yet the sky was not the limit, in terms of birthday gifts. In fact, the bank account was nearly empty. Louisa's marriage to Stephanie's father had gotten increasingly worse over the years and finally, in the past year, Louisa had felt that it would be best to split up. The divorce left Louisa strapped financially and anxious about expenses.

"Mommy," Stephanie signed one day, "I know what I want for my birthday." Louisa took a deep breath, worried that she would not be able to accommodate her daughter's wishes.

"Yes, honey," Louisa signed back, "what is it that you would like?"

"A white cat," Stephanie signed. A great big smile came over her face, just thinking about it. "A white female cat with long hair."

Louisa gulped hard. The divorce was still something that Stephanie had not fully understood. Plus, they had recently moved, and Stephanie was adjusting to a new environment and a new set of schoolmates. Any child would have been challenged; Stephanie had almost more than she could bear. It broke Louisa's heart to watch her daughter holding up with such grace and strength.

And yet, a long-haired cat? Louisa had an immediate sense that such an exotic animal would be costly. Over the next few days, she struggled with the dilemma every time she looked into her daughter's eyes. Just the idea of it seemed to give Stephanie a happier countenance. Never had Louisa seen her daughter want something this badly. In the end, Louisa was so moved by her daughter's deep desire for this cat that she resolved to find one.

Her first move was to look through the newspaper classifieds. Maybe someone was selling a cat that would fit Stephanie's dream. Maybe it wouldn't be that expensive. She found four ads for cats for sale, and circled them in red ink. She called the first number.

"Hi, I'm responding to your ad in the paper," Louisa said to the stranger who answered the phone.

"Yes, I am selling a cat," came the reply.

"What color is it?" asked Louisa, fingers crossed.

"It's a beautiful, all black, male cat."

Louisa's heart sank a little. The exact opposite of what Stephanie had asked for! "Oh . . . I'm sorry," she said. "I was looking for a white cat . . . female . . . thank you," she said and hung up. There were still more numbers to call. Louisa tried the next number. "Hi, I'm calling about the ad in the newspaper about a cat for sale?"

"Yes," came the reply, "I'm selling a beautiful short-haired white male cat." Once again, Louisa's heart sank as she thought about her daughter's bright eyes, her animated signing, her reluctance to hear of anything but a pure white, long-haired, female cat. "No, I'm sorry, that's not what I was looking for," replied Louisa.

Louisa continued to make phone calls for the rest of the afternoon. She found people selling orange tabbies and gray Siamese, but no long-haired fitting her daughter's specific description. Frustrated in her efforts, Louisa decided to ask her daughter if she might want a different type of cat—or even another birthday present altogether. But as she approached Stephanie's room, she caught a glimpse of the child signing to God. "Please God," she saw Stephanie pray, "please help my Mommy find me a white female long-haired cat. It's all that I want. Please. I know you have lots of those kind of cats. Please give my Mommy one." Louisa couldn't move. She just stood in the doorway, watching her child, tears welling up in her eyes. Then, slowly, she turned around, went back to her own room, and said her own prayer.

The next day Louisa was on the hunt again. She called yet another number listed in an ad from a different county newspaper. But all she got was the answering machine, so she left her number and waited to hear back.

That night she got a call. "Hello," said a woman on the other end of the line. "I'm returning your call about the ad I had placed in the newspaper."

"Yes," Louisa said, "would you please describe the cat to me?"

"Sure," said the woman. "The cat is pure white, long-haired and female."

Louisa jumped out of her seat. "I'll take it!" she screamed.

"Great," came the response, "that will be five hundred dollars."

"*What!*" shouted Louisa, "five hundred dollars?"

Trying to contain her disappointment, Louisa tried to explain the situation to the woman. "You see," she began, "my little girl is turning ten, and this is all that she had wanted. I can't afford much. I was hoping that maybe, somehow I would be able to give this to her. But five hundred dollars is too much. It's an amount I can't afford to spend."

Nevertheless, the woman could not be dissuaded from her price. Louisa thanked the woman anyhow for calling her back, and they both hung up.

Louisa felt more hopeless than ever. "Dear God," she implored, "my little girl is so alone in her deaf world, with her father gone and in a new home, I really want to be able to give her the gift she wants so badly. Please, help me find the kind of cat she's looking for.

Just as Louisa was completing her prayers, the phone rang. The woman with the white cat had been moved by Stephanie's story, she said, and she felt a change of heart. She was willing to reduce the price to three hundred dollars.

"Thank you so much," said Louisa sadly, "but even three hundred dollars is still way above and beyond what I can afford."

The woman must have sensed the sadness and despondency in Louisa's voice.

"You know . . . I do have another cat, a long-haired, perfectly white female cat that I can't seem to give away," she began.

"Oh? What do you mean? Why is that?" asked Louisa, perking up.

"Well, you see," said the woman, "this particular cat is deaf."

Louisa was speechless. After a moment of silence, she released a grateful sigh, and then came her exhilarated reply. "I'll take it," she said. "I will gladly take that cat."

❧

Comment

The sound of magic rings loud and clear, even in a silent world.

*C*harles Francis Coghlan was born on Prince Edward Island in 1841. He displayed exceptional dramatic ability as a boy and first appeared on the stage in London in 1860. In the years that followed he attained international fame as an actor and was considered one of the greatest Shakespearean performers of his day. Throughout his life, Prince Edward Island remained his home.

The actor was appearing in Galveston, Texas, when he died on November 27, 1889, after a short illness. His lead-lined coffin was placed in a granite vault in a Galveston cemetery.

On September 8, 1900, the great hurricane struck Galveston Island. The flood waters washed into the cemeteries and shattered vaults and disinterred the dead. The bodies of the long dead mingled with the newly dead. Coffins beat a dirge against uprooted tombstones, then floated out into the Gulf of Mexico to be scattered far and wide by the waves.

After the fury of the hurricane had been spent, a backwash carried the coffin of Charles Coghlan to the southeast. There it was caught by the West Indian current and carried into the Gulf Stream. It drifted around the tip of Florida and began moving north in the great oceanic river.

The Gulf Stream current moves rapidly, approximately seventy miles a day, and it is quite likely that the coffin moved with this current until it reached the vicinity of Newfoundland. There it was probably blown out of the current by a gale.

Once free of the Gulf Stream, it apparently drifted aimlessly off the eastern Canadian coast, subject to vagrant winds and waves. No one will ever know.

In October 1908, after a series of gales, several fishermen left Prince Edward Island to set their nets in the Gulf of St. Lawrence. They noticed a large box lying low in the water and drifting toward shore. They towed it to the beach.

Encrusted with sea mollusks and barnacles, it was obvious the box had been in the water a long time. They chipped away the thick crust of shells. It was a coffin containing the body of a middle-aged man. A silver plate gave his name as Charles Coghlan, a name well-known on the island.

Only a few miles away was the village where he had been born and raised. Only a few miles away was the home where he had rested between his extensive travels. With appropriate ceremony and honor, he was buried near the church where he had been baptized.

Across the trackless sea, Charles Coghlan had at last reached home to stay.

—*Alan Vaughan*

$\mathcal{I}$*n* 1984, Gertrude Levine of Queens, New York, received a phone call from the administrator of an older adults' summer camp where, she thought, her mother was safely ensconced.

"Mrs. Levine," the administrator said in a subdued voice, "I'm terribly sorry to have to tell you the tragic news, but your mother, Sarah Stern, just had a heart attack and died in the hospital. I'm so sorry—please accept my deepest condolences."

The telephone slipping from her hand, Gertrude slumped in her chair, dazed and stricken. It was incomprehensible . . . her beloved mother, dead. Especially since she had always been so robust and alive, so high-spirited and feisty. In contemplating her mother's advancing age, she had often reassured herself that Sarah Stern would give the Angel of Death a good run for his money!

"Mrs. Levine, Mrs. Levine," came the administrator's faint voice from the telephone receiver on the floor. "Are you still there?"

Gertrude retrieved the phone in slow motion, still muddled and disoriented. "Y-yes, I'm here," she responded numbly.

"Mrs. Levine, I feel terrible to throw this at you so suddenly, but someone has to come to identify the body."

"I don't think I can bear to do it; I'll send a close relative instead."

"That'll be fine, Mrs. Levine. And again, please accept our deepest condolences. Your mother was a very fine woman. She loved you so much. She talked about you all the time, always telling everyone what a marvelous daughter she had."

Gertrude bowed her head in sorrow. She was shattered by the loss of her beloved mother. At the funeral and later, during the first hours of the *shiva* (the Jewish mourning period of seven days), her tears flowed unrestrainedly. She told the family members who sat on the low mourning stools with her that the shock was too much for her to absorb.

Several hours after the *shiva* had begun, the phone rang and someone handed Gertrude the receiver.

A crisp operator's voice announced: "Collect phone call for Gertrude Levine from Sarah Stern. Will you accept the charges?"

"Collect phone call from *whom?*" Gertrude asked, befuddled.

"Sarah Stern," the operator repeated.

"Is this someone's sick idea of a joke?" Gertrude asked. "I just *buried* her!"

"Gertrude!" A beloved and very real voice suddenly came over the line, fretting, "I can't seem to adjust my medicine . . ."

It was her mother, Sarah Stern.

There had been *two* Sarah Sterns at the camp, and the wrong family had been notified! The relative sent to identify the body had been sickened by the sight of a corpse and had given it only a quick, perfunctory look. "Yeah, sure it's Sarah Stern," she had muttered hastily, eager to depart. Because coffins are always kept closed during Jewish funerals and Jewish law prohibits viewing of the body, the mistake was never uncovered. Consequently, a stranger was now lying in the family plot!

"You cannot imagine the emotional trauma," sighs Gertrude Levine in rueful recollection as she recounts the saga. "Thinking my mother is dead . . . all the pain and suffering . . . the stress of the funeral and the burial *and* the commencement of the *shiva* that followed. I won't even talk about the expense or the public embarrassment. But of course, all this faded into insignificance when I considered that my mother was very much alive."

But the story doesn't end here. When Gertrude called the children of the other Sarah Stern to offer her condolences and ask that the family make arrangements to transfer *their* mother's body out of *her* mother's burial plot, they refused!

"She's there already," they said, "let her be! Why should we go to all the bother of digging her up, buying a burial plot, and giving her another funeral? One is enough."

Gertrude was aghast at the suggestion. How could she allow a complete stranger to remain in her mother's burial plot, lying next to her deceased father? She begged the children to remove their mother's body, but they ignored her appeals. She had community leaders call on her behalf, but they remained intractable. Finally, with no other recourse left, Gertrude had a local rabbi call the family and threaten to obtain a court order forcing them to comply. It was this approach that finally worked.

"So are you at least going to give your mother a decent funeral?" Gertrude asked the family when arrangements for the body's removal had been made. To her horror, the children replied that a gravesite funeral would be sufficient.

"In that case I'm coming!" Gertrude said passionately, having become drawn into the drama of the late Mrs. Stern's life, and feeling fiercely protective of her honor.

Besides the immediate family, she was the only one there.

Watching the pitiful proceedings unfold at the stark and lonely graveside funeral, Gertrude Levine felt engulfed by an overwhelming sorrow for the life and death of the second Mrs. Stern. At the same time, she also experienced an epiphany, one that illuminated God's plan.

"I always wondered how and why the bizarre mix-up with my mother occurred," she reflects. "At the dismal funeral that wrenched my heart, I suddenly understood the larger picture."

"You know," she said to the children after the funeral, "your mother must have really been a very special woman or, at least once in her lifetime, done something extraordinary. Because *three hundred people* came to her funeral—thinking she was *my* mother—and paid her homage. Look at what kind of funeral you gave her now, and think about what kind of funeral she had as a result of the strange coincidence. God *wanted* her to have an honorable funeral, one that she obviously would never have been accorded otherwise, so He arranged for the coincidence to occur."

Six months later, Gertrude's own mother—the first Sarah Stern—died. Once again, she was given a beautiful funeral, but this time only a hundred people came.

Why the stunning decline in numbers?

"People were tired of going to her funeral!" sighs Gertrude Levine.

❦

*Comment*
When the dance of life confounds us and we're uncertain of the next step, we can pause and remember that the choreography of our existence is divine and purposeful.

*T*wice we had been burned by unsavory tenants living in the basement apartment of our home. The first miscreant robbed us of two thousand dollars, while the second rogue fled in the dark of night owing us back rent for several months. We also had a close brush with a third, who came to see the vacant apartment and expressed an immediate interest in taking it. Thank God for an inquisitive neighbor with a sharp eye and a loose tongue. As soon as he left, she raced across the street. "You know that man who just left your apartment?" she said. "He's wanted in Argentina for murder."

Alas, my husband and I are not wise in the ways of the world, and we are naive when it comes to people. This innocence, which has lasted long past our youth, has provided us with many unexpected blessings and interesting encounters, but it has also furnished us with an overabundant supply of trials, tribulations, and sheer unmitigated grief that we surely could have done without.

"Let's face it," I sighed one day to my husband, as we thought forlornly about the basement apartment, which was—surprise!—vacant again. "The basement is very small and dingy. It only attracts real problematic and troublesome individuals. Let's call it quits as a rental and use it as a playroom for the kids."

"No way," he shook his head adamantly. "We put in a lot of money to fix it up and we need the income it provides."

"It's not worth the trouble!" I argued. "The apartment doesn't appeal to nice, quiet, respectable people. I shudder when I think that we almost harbored a *murderer* in our very own home!"

"We need the income!" my husband replied stubbornly.

"Can you promise me you'll be extremely careful in checking out the next tenant? Ask for references and so on?"

"I promise. And I'll tell you what. Just to really be on the safe side, I'll try to rent the apartment to a woman rather than a man. Okay?"

"If it doesn't work out this time, I want you to promise me never again," I warned.

"No more heartache," he promised cheerfully.

When an elegantly dressed middle-aged schoolteacher appeared several days later and expressed an interest in renting the apartment, my husband excitedly gave her a lease on the spot and called the local newspaper to cancel the ad he had placed.

"You'll love her!" he assured me, when I expressed my dubiousness about the deal.

"I don't understand this," I said warily. "Why would a well-heeled schoolteacher choose *our* apartment? It doesn't make any sense. Did you ask her for references?"

"She's so respectable looking, I didn't want to insult her by asking for references."

"*What?*" I shrieked. "I don't believe this. You promised."

"I know people," he said confidently. "This is a fine woman. You'll see."

One week later, a moving van appeared in front of our house, and movers began heaving furniture into the basement apartment. I looked for the elegant woman my husband had described, but the person directing the movers with an authoritative air was a young man, neatly dressed in a decent suit. I approached him and asked if he was related to the new tenant.

"That's my mother," he said, flashing a bright, charming smile. "She went abroad for a few weeks, but she said I could use her apartment while she's gone."

The young man looked respectable enough, although I was a little unnerved by his long ponytail and his earring. However, always having given my children long-drawn-out lectures about the importance of looking beyond outward appearances, I was embarrassed not to try to practice what I preached.

"I guess it's OK," I responded. "When is she coming back?"

"Soon," he answered vaguely.

The woman never materialized.

After the first day, the suit never materialized again either. Instead, the new tenant began appearing regularly in torn jeans and tight-fitting T-shirts. A few weeks later, the T-shirt was replaced by an undershirt, and soon after that, he began walking around with a bare chest that exposed several ominous-looking tattoos.

Soon, bizarre-looking characters began drifting in and out of our basement apartment and raucous music could be heard late at night. My husband tracked down the mysterious woman, who confessed that she had tricked him into renting the apartment to her problematic son, Michael.

"I'm sorry," she said, not sounding sorry at all. "But nobody wanted to rent him an apartment, so I had to do it for him. He's a good boy, don't worry. He won't hurt you."

"Can't we get Michael out?" I wailed to my husband day in and day out.

"Even if we have legal recourse, it'll take months. Anyway," my Good Samaritan husband gently chastened me, "instead of focusing on Michael's problems, maybe we should see the situation in a different context. Maybe it's no accident that he landed here, since we've worked with people like him in the past. See it as a test from God," my husband counseled. "Let's invite him for Friday night Sabbath dinner."

Friday night, Michael gleamed like the silver candlesticks on my resplendently set Sabbath table. He wore the first day's suit, and was buffed and polished handsomely. He wore a *yarmulke* out of respect for our Orthodox tradition. (He was Jewish but not religious.)

He helped me serve dinner, engaged in witty, charming banter with my sons, told a few jokes, sang a few Jewish melodies in an enchanting baritone, and even recounted a few Hasidic tales that he remembered from his childhood days.

"Do you see the beauty in this boy's soul?" my husband pressed me after he left. "We can do good work here."

A few weeks later, we found out that Michael was a drug addict.

"Now what?" I sighed to my husband.

"Well, the challenge is *bigger* now, but I still believe we can help him. Now I really know his coming here was no accident. God sent him to us and we've got to help him."

Truly I felt conflicted. On the one hand, I agreed with my husband. On the other hand, I didn't feel that we were equipped to deal with a drug problem. Most important, I worried about my children's safety and the safety of the other children on the block. My husband had confronted Michael about his addiction and he swore he would hide his problem from them. He also gave my husband his word that he would enter a drug rehabilitation program and said that he had already applied to one in California. He also told my husband that as a result of our influence he had started attending synagogue and was thinking about becoming observant. He had even sent away for information about schools that specialized in returnees to Judaism, he said.

My husband was satisfied. He didn't entertain for a moment the thought of having Michael evicted, as I had half-hoped he would. Whether Michael was sincere about his intentions or fed my husband the lines he knew would push his buttons, I couldn't be sure. But his promises certainly kept the sheriff's men at bay.

One night, I drove to Brooklyn Heights, a neighborhood about thirty minutes from where I live, to take an adult education course. The class ended at eleven, and I asked the instructor for directions back to the highway. I was a trifle nervous about driving home alone late at night, but once I got onto the highway, I breathed a sigh of relief. It would be smooth sailing from here on, I thought.

My relief was premature. To my distress, I suddenly realized that I was on the wrong side of the highway. I was on my way to *Queens* instead of Brooklyn! I had no recourse but to get off the highway immediately. At the next exit sign, I pulled off the ramp and began searching for an entrance to the Brooklyn-bound side.

I was dazed and disoriented. It would have been a strain even during the daytime, but the misshapen shadows of the night played into my fears. These fears were heightened and compounded by my sudden realization that I was cruising along the streets of one of the toughest neighborhoods in Brooklyn.

"It's OK. Nothing's going to happen," I reassured myself, repeating the words like a mantra. "Just find a gas station and the attendant will give you directions."

A gas station appeared around a bend. Weak with relief, I pulled into it and honked my horn. Anticipating that the attendant would be out momentarily, I rolled down my window to talk with him. Instead, five menacing figures stepped out of the station's shadows and encircled my car. The attendant was nowhere to be seen.

"Need help, lady?" one man growled, as I cautioned myself to look beyond appearances.

"Hi, good evening, how ya doing?" I said brightly, deciding that the cool I'm-not-scared-of-you, you-are-God's-divine-creature-just-as-much-as-I-am approach might work here. "Could you please tell me how to get onto the BQE going west?"

"Sure, honey, I'll be glad to," the man said, and for a fraction of a second my fears were allayed. "But it'll cost you . . . " he added with a growl.

The menacing figures moved closer to the car.

Suddenly, a new figure detached itself from another throng of men huddled in a corner of the gas station and raced towards my car. "I recognize that voice. It's Mrs. Mandelbaum! Mrs. Mandelbaum, Mrs. Mandelbaum, how ya doin'!" the voice inquired serendipitously.

It was Michael.

He approached the men encircling the car and scowled at them threateningly. "What're you bothering this nice lady for? She's my landlady. Leave her alone! Scram!"

Reluctantly, the men walked away from the car, giving it and me one last lingering look.

"Mrs. Mandelbaum, what are you doing here?" my savior inquired blithely.

"Michael, what are *you* doing here?" I countered.

"Oh, I come here to do some business," he answered vaguely.

"Want a lift home?" I asked.

"Nah, thanks, but I'm not finished here yet."

"Michael, you probably saved my life. I don't know how to thank you."

"Well, you've been valiantly trying to save mine, so I guess we're even now," he said in a light tone.

A few weeks after the gas station incident, Michael left for a rehabilitation center in California. I haven't seen him since, but I pray that God will continue to protect the man who protected me the night I took a wrong turn off the highway.

— *Yitta Halberstam Mandelbaum*

$\mathcal{I}n$ New York City, the police advise you not to take out your wallet when approached by a beggar—but you develop a sixth sense about these things. So I had no misgivings about the young black woman, shy and rail-thin and obviously homeless, her matted hair covered by a scarf, who approached me a few years ago in the nearly empty Times Square subway station while I was waiting for the train.

Could I give her some money for a meal?

I took a few dollars from my wallet. Then I noticed her feet. She was wearing threadbare sneakers and had no socks on. I asked her why. She had no money for socks, she explained as she turned to ask another commuter for spare change.

I had no more money to offer. But the vision of her sockless feet accompanied me home. I rummaged through my dresser drawers for a few pairs of nearly new, thick socks and put them in a plastic bag.

I waited for the woman for the next several days in the same place, at the same time, but she never showed up. Unwilling to give up, unable to linger on the platform, I brought my little package up a flight of stairs to the woman who worked in the token booth. Though we had never spoken, we did have a smiling relationship. I usually traveled to and from Manhattan before rush hour, and she knew my face.

I asked the clerk to open the booth's side door. I handed her the bag and an assignment: Please be on the lookout for a thin, black homeless woman who comes to the station in mid-afternoon and has no socks. And give her these socks.

My schedule kept me from that subway station for the next several weeks. When I finally went by her booth again, the clerk excitedly waved me over.

No, the young homeless woman had never showed up. But, the clerk told me, the day after I left the bag two homeless men knocked on the booth's door and said their socks were wet. Their feet were cold. Did she have any dry socks?

She gave the men my package.

She had never seen those men before, she said. She had worked at that station for several years, and no one had ever asked her for socks before.

"The Lord," she said, "sure works in mysterious ways."

— *Steve Lipman*

#### Comment

Our good intentions are powerful enough to set the wheel of miracles in motion.

*J*ohn Donovan's father was a cantankerous, ornery fellow whose querulous temperament had alienated many friends, relatives, and neighbors over the years, literally driving them away. His churlish manner had worsened with advancing age and chronic illness, and he was cross and disagreeable all the time now. Hence, John Donovan found it virtually impossible to find live-in help for his father—something that had become an absolute necessity since his mother had died two years before.

The city he lived in abounded in home-attendant agencies that catered to people like his father, and good, reliable help was easy to come by. But nobody stayed for more than a week.

The routine was always the same. The new prospect would arrive with shining eyes and a determined manner, and John would warn, cautiously, "My father is not an easy man." The home attendant would shrug, smile, and say something reassuring like, "No one who is sick and elderly is easy." But a week later, the smile would be wiped off, replaced by a grimace of pain, and the shining eyes would have become weary and bloodshot. "Sorry," they would say quickly, as they beat a hasty retreat. "But your father is just impossible."

John Donovan couldn't blame them. *He* couldn't wait to retreat from his father's presence, either. No matter what or how much he did for him, his father always grumbled and complained.

"There has to be someone who exists in this world who could have a magical effect on Dad!" John said in exasperation one day. "Someone like Mom," he added wistfully.

Indeed, his sweet, soft-spoken mother had always had a calming influence on his truculent father. People had marveled for years about the way he became transformed when she was around. "He's like a different person altogether," they would often remark.

If people had physical doubles in the world, why couldn't they have emotional ones? Why couldn't he find a home attendant with a serene temperament and a mellow nature, someone who mirrored his mother completely?

"Oh, Mom!" he cried at her grave one day. "I know this is the height of desperation, coming to ask you for help. But I'm at my wit's end. Please send me a home attendant for Dad—someone just like you!"

"I can't believe what I just did!" John thought as he walked away from the grave, rubbing his forehead in disbelief. "Praying at a parent's grave for good health or general success is one thing. But praying for a home attendant is downright ridiculous!"

Still, when the phone rang two days later, John couldn't help but wonder if there wasn't a connection.

"Mr. Donovan," chirped a pleasant-sounding voice. "Mrs. O'Reilley here. I think I've finally hit pay dirt.

There's a young man looking for a home attendant position who fits the bill perfectly. I think you'll be very pleased."

His name was Charlie Edwards and he was planning to be a nurse one day. In the meantime, he was saving for his tuition by working as an attendant, and he had walked into the agency for the first time that morning.

Although easygoing and placid in temperament, Charlie possessed a wicked sense of humor, a mischievous smile, and an infectious, boisterous laugh that engaged everyone, including (despite himself) John Donovan's father. It was virtually impossible not to be charmed by Charlie's warmth and winsome appeal. In truth, he *was* just like John's mother, and John was pretty much convinced that somehow she had arranged this match, just the way he had asked her to.

So, for the second time that week, John Donovan journeyed to his mother's grave—this time to express his profound appreciation for her very efficient manner of granting his request. After praying at her gravesite for several minutes, he murmured his thanks for her rapid intercession and then began to talk out loud to her, as he always did, in the teasing, jocular manner he had adopted with her since he was a teenager. "So, gee Mom, I hope you have good company around here. . . . Any interesting neighbors?"

He didn't know where the impulse to ask came from. He had never given the neighboring tombstones even a passing glance. But this time his eyes involuntarily flickered to the gravestone immediately adjoining his mother's. His eyes widened. "Now, that's interesting," he muttered to himself. "Wonder if he's related? . . . Nah, what's the big deal?" he said dismissively. "It's a very common name, very common."

"Hey, Charlie," John said in conversation a few days later. "I know this is a long shot, but are you by any chance related to someone named Wayne Edwards?"

"Yes, I am, but Edwards is a common name, and we're probably not talking about the same guy anyway."

"Why do you say that?" pressed John.

"Because the Wayne Edwards I knew is long dead and buried."

"And is he by any chance currently residing in the All-Saints Cemetery?" asked John.

"How'd you know that?" asked Charlie with a puzzled frown.

"Wayne Edwards is buried right next to my mother. Charlie," exclaimed John with mounting excitement, "who *was* Wayne Edwards?"

Charlie turned to John, his complexion ashen but his eyes ablaze with wonder.

"John," he answered slowly, "Wayne Edwards was my *grandfather.*"

**"Obviously,"** Charlie mused, "this was a match made in heaven!"

*W*hen Heather McCarty became engaged in 1971, she was delighted with the beautiful diamond ring her fiancé presented to her, and didn't anticipate that any more extravagant gifts or expensive pieces of jewelry would be coming her way. After all, her prospective groom was a struggling young man in his early twenties, and the diamond ring had been costly. So she was surprised and pleased when he arrived at her home one evening proudly bearing aloft a jeweler's box containing yet another gift.

"Oh, you shouldn't have!" she gurgled delightedly as she tore the gift wrap off the box and opened it. Nestled inside was an heirloom antique pin, a large gold cameo inlaid with emerald and cobalt stones, with a second, smaller cameo dangling from it. The second cameo was an exact replica of the first.

As soon as she saw the pin, Heather's heart sank and her delight turned to chagrin, which she valiantly tried to conceal. She didn't want to hurt her fiancé's feelings, but the pin was wrong for her, all wrong. First, she was a small-boned, petite woman only five feet tall, and the pin was very large and would engulf her. Second, her taste leaned towards the more modest and conservative, and the pin was gaudy and ostentatious. What was the point of accepting the gift if she was never going to wear it?

"You know," her fiancé told her proudly, "the jeweler I bought this from says it's a one-of-a-kind piece. It was purchased as part of an estate sale, and it was custom-made for the original owner. There's not a pin like this anywhere else in the world!"

Gently, Heather told her fiancé that although she treasured his good intentions and the sentiment that made him buy it, the piece wasn't for her. "Do you mind if I go back with you to the jeweler and exchange the pin for something else?" she asked.

He was disappointed but indulgent. The jeweler, however, was not as accommodating. "You don't like this pin?" he asked, astonished. "It's a magnificent piece — one of a kind! What don't you like about it exactly?"

Heather explained that the pin was simply "too much" for her small frame and simple tastes — but the jeweler wouldn't hear of it. He persisted tenaciously in his efforts to get her to keep the piece. He was a strong and forceful person, and he tried his best to impose his will on Heather, but she was no pushover either, and they remained locked in a stalemate.

Finally, the jeweler shouted in elation: "Why didn't I think of this before? I have the perfect solution! Let me remove the second miniature 'baby' cameo pin that dangles from the larger 'mother' one. This will make the pin smaller and less flashy. What do you say?"

"Well . . ." said Heather dubiously.

"Look," said the jeweler quickly, "let me do it for you right now on the spot, and if you don't like the way it looks minus the second pin, I won't say another word." And deftly, he extracted a jeweler's tool from his pouch and the deed was done.

By itself, the "mother" pin was certainly less flamboyant and more in keeping with Heather's taste. It was still a little garish but definitely more discreet-looking with the replica removed.

"Okay," said Heather to the jeweler. "I can live with it now. I'll keep it. . . . So what are you going to do with the miniature cameo?" she asked as an afterthought as she prepared to leave.

"Oh, it's no problem," he answered. "It stands on its own. I can definitely sell it as a separate piece. Don't you worry about it; I'll sell it in a snap."

Over the years, Heather kept the pin in a bank vault, removing it only to wear on special occasions. She had never quite made peace with its flamboyant air, and only wore it at formal black-tie affairs. Whenever she did wear it, though, she could not help but think about the second cameo that had been separated from the larger piece. "It definitely looks as though something is missing from it," she would often muse, and she would wonder who owned the smaller piece now.

Twenty-one years later, Heather's daughter Micky became engaged. Her fiancé, a struggling young man in his early twenties, presented her with a diamond ring, and Micky expected nothing more.

But one evening, her fiancé came to her home, proudly bearing aloft a small jeweler's box.

Nestled inside was the second "baby" cameo pin. After two decades it had journeyed back to its source, thereby creating a true "mother and child" reunion.

"Millions of New Yorkers, millions of pieces of jewelry in the world," muses Heather. "My future son-in-law had never seen me wear the mother piece, didn't even know I owned it. How could this have happened? I'm still not sure what it meant, but for my daughter, the interpretation was clear. When she saw the pin nestled in the box, any qualms she might have had about the engagement vanished. For her, the pin's reappearance in our lives was a sign. It augured positive things, and a sense of destiny. In a word, it sealed the deal."

❧

### Comment
Since everything in this universe contains a spark of divinity, everything plays a role in the divine plan.

*M*ichael Yaeger was driving his elderly father Morris to his summer cottage in a mountain resort, when the older man began speaking of the mysterious moments he had encountered during his life. One particular incident stood out in his memory, and he began to regale Michael with details of the event.

"In 1929," he reminisced, "I attended the funeral of my grandfather, Yeshaya Sholom Gross, known throughout Hungary as a very holy man. Thousands of people were in attendance at this funeral, which was held in the Jewish cemetery in Budapest. Just as the graveside ceremony was about to begin, a big, white, unusual-looking bird swooped down from the sky, alighted on the coffin, and squatted there, almost as if it had come to join in the proceedings. The people at the cemetery were riveted by the sight, not only because the bird was unusual-looking but also because it seemed rooted to its spot.

"Perched on the coffin, the bird didn't move from its position once, but sat there quiet and unblinking.

"Despite their grief, the people in the crowd couldn't help but glance at the bird as speaker after speaker rose to eulogize the great sage. They pointed and whispered. *Was it still there? It was. Still? Yes. How long had it been? Hours.*

*"Was it conceivable that the bird had come to pay homage to the Holy Man? Who knew? Could the bird be a* gilgul —a *reincarnation? Could be. Maybe the sage once helped a bird? Anything was possible.*

"The whispers got louder at the conclusion of the funeral. For at the precise moment that the ceremony came to an official end and the coffin was about to be lowered into the ground, the bird darted a quick look around the cemetery, flapped its wings, and flew onto a nearby tombstone. It continued to squat there until my grandfather was buried. It was only after the masses had filed out of the cemetery that the bird finally soared into the sky and disappeared from view.

"It had sat immobile during the entire funeral—three hours long.

"So, what do you make of this story?" Morris Yaeger demanded of his son as he finished the tale.

Michael Yaeger, a cerebral sort who embraced the rational and eschewed the mystical, laughed.

"That's a ridiculous story!" he scoffed. "It can't possibly be true. You're making it up. Or exaggerating. The bird probably sat on the coffin for a short period. In your grief, your sense of time became warped. No, I don't believe this story for a minute," he said dismissively.

Just then, a big, white, unusual-looking bird swooped down from the sky and perched on the hood of the car. Michael looked at the bird in disbelief, waiting for it to fly away as suddenly and abruptly as it had descended.

It didn't move.

Throughout the rest of the two-and-a-half-hour journey from New York City to upstate New York, the bird sat still and unblinking on its roost on the hood of the car. No matter how much Michael speeded up, and despite all the bumps and curves on the road, the bird steadfastly clung to its perch on the car, and it stayed there until their journey's end.

When the Yaegers reached their destination in the countryside, the bird darted a quick glance in their direction and then soared away.

❧

### Comment

Messengers do not always assume human shape. Validation may come in many forms; but only if we are open to the mysteries of the universe can we fully receive its blessings.

*S*heroll Carby was a social worker at the Saint William's Center in Louisville, Kentucky. As part of her duties, Sheroll regularly made home visits, checking on her clients and tending to their needs.

On one of her weekly visits not long ago, Sheroll went to see one of her favorites, Joseph Wilson, a handsome elderly man with a delicate face framed by a full head of white hair. Sitting in his living room, she addressed his health concerns and discussed his poor eating habits. Suddenly, much to her surprise, she caught sight of a small pistol with a pearl handle lying on the couch beside him.

Trying to act nonchalant, she forced herself to interrupt their regular conversation. "Uh . . . Mr. Wilson," she stuttered, "what is that object beside your hip? Is it what I think it is? It can't be real." Sheroll was surprised—to put it mildly—that gentle old Mr. Wilson would possess such a weapon. Or any weapon.

"Yes, it's for real," said Mr. Wilson in a matter-of-fact manner. "I keep it for protection."

Sheroll was alarmed. She tried to understand his reasoning. She asked, "Is it necessary to keep it out in the open like that?"

"I hope it doesn't bother you. I don't remember why I left it out in plain sight," he replied. "Usually I hide it. I even sleep with it under my pillow."

Sheroll didn't know how to respond to this. She imagined the gun going off accidentally while he slept. After a brief silence she asked: "Is it loaded?"

"Well, honey," he said with some sarcasm, "it ain't much good if it ain't loaded."

Social workers, Sheroll realized, often encountered strange situations. Seeing Mr. Wilson's gun disturbed her. She managed to muster up the nerve to ask a question to which, she was sure, she would get a flat *no!*

"Can I have your bullets?" Sheroll asked.

To her complete surprise, he said, "I guess so." And with that, he handed her the gun. Sheroll tried to pry open the pistol. She had no idea what she was doing. She naively took a screwdriver to open the chamber and remove the bullets.

With the bullets dislodged, Sheroll felt somewhat better. She completed her unusual visit with Mr. Wilson and drove home. She was relieved to find her husband there, home early from the office. She told him about her bizarre visit with Mr. Wilson, and about how she had removed the bullets from the gun. He didn't seem the least bit concerned. "He'll probably reload the gun anyway," he said. Sheroll felt annoyed at her husband's casual attitude.

"I don't have any right to take the gun away, do I?" she asked. That ended the conversation, but the thought did not leave her mind. The image of Mr. Wilson and his gun kept coming back to her. She dreamed about it all that night. The next day, while on her way to other clients, Sheroll could not stop thinking about Mr. Wilson and his pistol. Her next visit with him was scheduled for the end of the week. However, she felt compelled to go back and confront him again. She turned the car around and made an impromptu appearance, catching Mr. Wilson unawares.

She got directly to the point. "Mr. Wilson," Sheroll asked, "did you reload the gun after I left last night?"

"Why, of course I did," he replied openly.

"It really bothers me," said Sheroll. "Did it ever occur to you what might happen if someone stole your pistol? A crime could be committed with it."

"Well, I never thought about it in that light," he answered, stroking his chin.

All at once Sheroll found herself asking a question that sounded naive. "Can I keep the gun and put it somewhere for safekeeping?"

Again, to her complete surprise, he said, "Sure, you can *have* the gun."

Feeling uneasy about taking the pistol, she was nevertheless relieved that he relinquished it so easily. As soon as she left, Sheroll took the gun over to the nearest police station and had them put it in the property room.

Late the next afternoon, right before her office closed, Sheroll picked up the ringing phone. It was Mr. Wilson.

"You won't believe what happened!" he exclaimed. Sheroll heard the agitation in his voice and listened with bated breath. "Right after you left, a guy came to my door. Everyone in the neighborhood knows him as a junkie hooked on drugs. He crashed through my front door and started punching me. I fell to the floor on both knees. Then he ransacked my place and put a few things in his satchel. Nothing of real value, though. Suddenly he got really agitated and started to look under my pillow and mattress. I don't know what he expected to find, but I bet it was my gun."

Sheroll listened intently to every word. "You must be my guardian angel," continued Mr. Wilson, his voice calming down as he spoke. "I don't remember how long I've owned that pistol. But thank God you took it away from me when you did. There's no telling what he would have done if he'd found it. More than likely he would have shot me."

♾

### Comment
When we show care and concern for others, violence dissolves and love, peace, and harmony grow in its stead.

*Finding* a penny is supposed to bring good luck. Sharon Kovalsky found considerably more than a penny. Within two weeks, her discovery would pay her a very valuable dividend.

Sharon's good luck originated in the fast checkout line at the Super Duper Supermarket in Rochester, New York. While standing on line with her few purchases, she felt a lump under her right foot. She looked down. There on the floor was a wrinkled ten-dollar bill. She stooped down immediately to pick it up.

Her first impulse was to hand it over to the checkout clerk. On second thought, she quickly pulled back the money in her clutched hand. "He'll probably pocket it himself," she thought. Then another, more pragmatic option came to mind. "I think I'll keep it safe for awhile instead. I don't need it now. Who knows, maybe I'll get a chance to put it to good use later," she told herself. With that, she tucked the bill into a "safety" compartment in her wallet. She had never used that compartment before. She was pleased with her quick decision, which would let her forget the whole matter until the right time and place came along. With a smile on her face, she paid for her groceries and drove home.

Two weeks later Sharon found herself in the very same checkout line. Although she had only three items in her basket, she waited patiently behind an elderly woman, shabbily dressed. The temperature was frigid outside. Sharon felt compassion for this shivering woman whose face bore the telltale lines of many years of struggling to make ends meet. The cashier rang up her meager sale and was waiting impatiently to be paid. Sharon looked at the woman with complete sympathy. Then Sharon's chain of thought was interrupted when she heard the woman speak.

"Two weeks ago when I was here," she said to the clerk as her arthritic fingers rummaged through her empty purse, "I lost a ten-dollar bill. I don't have enough money now to pay for these few things."

What an extraordinary coincidence. "I can't believe my ears," Sharon said to herself. "This has to be the moment I've been waiting for." She immediately unzipped the safety compartment of the wallet she had in her hand.

To get the old woman's attention, Sharon tapped her on the shoulder. "Two weeks ago I was here, too, madam, and I found this ten-dollar bill on the floor." Without a moment's hesitation, Sharon pulled out her "lucky" find—the very bill the old woman had dropped.

*J*ohn Evans* was in a foul mood. The grimy sink was overflowing with dirty dishes, toys were strewn around the kitchen floor, piles of musty newspapers were heaped on the dining room table, and stacks of laundry waiting to be sorted lay silently in rebuke on the living room couch. From the children's bedrooms came a cacophony of wild shrieks and loud music. "I can't cope with all of this!" John thought, frustrated and angry at himself for not being able to manage the chaos that had overtaken his home. "How did Heather handle the kids and the house so perfectly?" he asked himself in awe. "She always seemed to be in total control."

Heather, his adored wife of seventeen years, had died three months before of breast cancer. John had been devastated by her death, but didn't have the time to mourn properly. He had been left with six children ranging in age from three to fifteen, and he could only afford a part-time housekeeper to come in a couple of times a week to give him a hand. He held a demanding job as an accountant in a big firm, and tax season was at hand. It was all he could do to maintain his workload and keep some semblance of order at home. He was beginning to feel as if he would break.

"Let's play hide and seek!" cried the two youngest children, three-year-old Todd and four-year-old Tracy, as they darted into the living room, oblivious of their father seated at his desk.

"You hide first!" commanded the older child. "I'll count . . . one, two, three, four . . . ready or not, here I come!"

"Dad . . ." Fifteen-year-old Jeff wandered into the room. "Have you seen my Meat Loaf CD?"

"Dad," Susie called from her room where she was working on a book report, "can you give me some help here?"

"Daddy . . ." Eight-year-old Jeff tugged at his arm. "I don't understand my math homework. Can you explain it to me?"

"Daddy!" shouted Tracy as she returned to the living room, scowling. "I can't find Todd anywhere. Have you seen him?"

"Aren't you guys playing hide and seek?" John said absently, rubbing his temples, where a vein was beginning to throb.

"Yeah, we are. But where could he be? I've looked everywhere."

"Just keep on looking, honey. He probably found a great place you didn't think of," answered John as he went to answer the doorbell.

A panhandler was standing on the steps.

"Yeah?" John grunted ungraciously.

"Good afternoon!" the man said brightly. "Mrs. Evans in?"

"Mrs. Evans is dead."

"Ohmygod!" the man clutched his heart in shock. "What happened? . . . I'm so sorry. . . . What a great lady. . . . What happened?"

"Breast cancer," John barked.

"Daddy! Daddy!" Tracy ran to the door, pulling at John's sleeve with urgency. "I *still* can't find Todd. I've looked everywhere!"

"Honey," John answered impatiently, "the front door was locked when I opened it now. He didn't leave the house. He's here somewhere. He's a tiny kid, he probably squeezed into a place you wouldn't think of yourself. You just have to look harder!"

"Listen," he said as he turned to the panhandler, "I'm really sorry, but I can't talk right now. . . . I've got tons of things to do; I'm up to my neck. Here!" And he thrust two dollars into the panhandler's palm.

"Uhh . . . Mr. Evans . . ." The panhandler shifted uncomfortably. "Sorry to bother you at a difficult time like this, but I wonder if I might have something to eat?"

"What do you think the two dollars is supposed to be for . . . booze?" John asked rudely.

"Mr. Evans," the panhandler said, looking at him chidingly. "Your wife was a very special woman. Whenever I came to the door, she never gave me less than ten dollars. *And* she always invited me in for a full, hot meal. I will never forget her kindness. I owe her a great debt."

"Well, I'm not my wife," John snapped.

"Mr. Evans," the panhandler entreated. "I haven't eaten in a day. Surely you have something in the fridge that you can spare?"

"All right, come in," John said grudgingly.

As he ushered the man into the living room, he caught sight of Tracy peering under the couch.

"Still can't find him, hon?" he asked.

"Dad . . . it's been so long . . . why hasn't Todd come out of his hiding place yet? . . . I'm worried."

"Please, Mr. Evans . . . I'm so hungry!" interjected the panhandler.

"Well, wherever Todd is, he definitely deserves a prize for outwitting you for so long, doesn't he?" John said distractedly to Tracy as he headed for the kitchen.

He opened the refrigerator and there, curled up inside, blue and unconscious, was Todd.

"You found him not a moment too soon," the hospital staff doctor told him later in the emergency room. "Probably just a few minutes more in the refrigerator and he would have been a goner for sure. What luck that you discovered him when you did! We've revived him and he'll be fine."

"Whoever was hungry at that particular moment," the doctor laughed over his shoulder as he walked away, "saved your son's life!"

*R*osemary Macri was eight months pregnant when the baby suddenly showed signs of heart distress. "Will my baby be all right?" she asked, as she lay in New York Hospital's maternity ward, hooked up to machines she could barely comprehend. "We'll do the best we can," responded the doctor. "But I have to be honest with you—there is only so much we can do."

A legion of doctors and nurses kept vigil over the fetus during the next twenty-four hours. But despite their efforts, the baby's condition worsened. The doctors made a decision to induce labor. Shortly thereafter, Rosemary gave birth to a baby boy.

For what seemed like an eternity, Rosemary lay waiting for her child's prognosis. She watched the nurses come and go from their stations. She heard the sound of technology and television. She smelled disinfectant. Finally, overcome with weariness and numb with shock, she fell into a deep sleep.

As Rosemary slept, the staff was very concerned about the poor prognosis of Rosemary's newborn. They knew all too well the grave odds against the baby's survival. They called in the priest. "The mother is fast asleep," the priest said, "and it is my belief that given the circumstances, the child should be baptized." Right there and then, the child was baptized.

All the while, Rosemary slumbered peacefully. In her dreams, a vision of her late Uncle Patrick appeared. "Don't worry," the calming voice said, "your child will be well. Everything will be fine."

Just as the ad hoc baptism came to an end, Rosemary awoke from her deep state of slumber. The dream about her uncle, and the soothing words he had spoken, had made her feel comforted. But now her own heart froze with terror when she saw the priest. He must have known, for he spoke quickly. "My dear," he said, "hold on to hope because the situation has been so precarious, we baptized the baby. We named him Patrick."

She was just opening her mouth to speak to the priest, to tell him about her dream, when the doctors entered the room. The priest and Rosemary looked at them pleadingly. "Your son will be just fine."

*J*erry Simon\* first met Yehuda Finerman\* at a kibbutz in Israel. The young Simon had fled there after a brief stint in the U.S. Army, where he had encountered subtle and not-so-subtle forms of anti-Semitism. "Just a few short years after World War II," Jerry had thought in anguish, "and nobody seems to have learned any lessons. What kind of world do we live in?"

So he escaped to a different kind of world—a world that had captured the imagination of quixotic idealists and bold adventurers alike; a world that beckoned those who were disillusioned with the rat race and the dog-eat-dog existence of contemporary life: the seemingly idyllic world of the Israeli kibbutz.

In the early days of the Jewish state, Simon was one of thousands of foreigners who volunteered to work on a kibbutz, and it was there that he met Finerman, a European immigrant who had survived the Holocaust. Finerman was close-mouthed about the horrors he had endured, and Jerry discreetly avoided the subject.

But one hot summer day, when the two were toiling side by side in the kibbutz fields under the blazing sun and Finerman's shirtsleeves were rolled up high, Jerry could not help but notice the numbers tattooed on his friend's forearm. And when he had registered these numbers, he could not help but emit an audible gasp.

"What's the matter, Jerry?" Finerman asked.

"I—I'm sorry, Yehuda," Jerry stammered, "I'm not trying to be nosy or anything, but I couldn't help but notice the numbers on your forearm."

"Surely you've seen them on other survivors before," Finerman responded curtly.

"Of course I have. It's—it's just . . . well, what struck me as odd is that your concentration camp numbers—7416—just happen to be the last four digits of my American social security number!"

"That's what you're excited about?" Finerman scoffed. "It's just a meaningless coincidence!"

"Look, Yehuda," Jerry pleaded. "I know it's hard for you . . . but I care about you . . . deeply. Could you tell me how you got those numbers?"

Finerman looked at Jerry thoughtfully. "Maybe it *is* a mistake for survivors to hide their experiences from the rest of the world. Maybe we *were* meant to serve as witnesses. . . . All right, Jerry, I'll tell you exactly what happened."

And the two sat down in the fields under the blazing sun and Finerman recounted a story that was familiar and yet not familiar in its telling—a story that was his but not his alone.

". . . And then," an hour later Yehuda concluded, "we stood on line at selection . . . my brothers, my sisters, my parents, and I . . . and we were branded with these concentration camp numbers . . . in numerical order. . . . I was next to last, followed by my brother. Afterward, we were split up, and I never saw any of them again. I was the only one in my family who survived the war."

Jerry was silent when Yehuda's recital of the terrors he had suffered came to an abrupt end. In the face of such suffering, what could he possibly say? Now he understood why survivors were so loath to recount their stories. Their nightmare was truly unutterable, unspeakable—and words were impotent in imparting the full extent of the nightmare. But the story had to be told, didn't it?

Many years later, Jerry left the kibbutz and began working in the Jerusalem–Tel Aviv area as a tour guide for wealthy Americans who wanted to be personally chaperoned around Israel in a comfortable limousine. Most of his clients were kind and amiable, and Jerry generally enjoyed his job. But one day, he picked up a new client at the airport whose behavior was downright insufferable.

The man was domineering, rude, gruff, and harsh. He was a control freak, and continually shouted orders and commands at Jerry from the passenger seat in the back. Jerry clenched his teeth and made an almost superhuman effort to remain polite. Finally, just when he felt he couldn't take it anymore, the man inexplicably shouted: "Pull to the side of the road!"

"What?" Jerry asked, confused.

"I said pull to the side of the road! . . . Look," said the man to Jerry, who had turned around to face his tormentor, "you don't like me very much, do you?"

Jerry was silent.

"I know sometimes my behavior is obnoxious, offensive. Sometimes even I can't quite believe myself what I've become. I'm sorry; I apologize. It's just that . . . it's just that . . . I'm so alone in the world; I've endured so much . . . there are nights I think I just won't make it through . . ."

And then the man broke down and cried. "You think I'm an arrogant, wealthy American businessman," he said to Jerry. "What I really am," he sobbed, "is a Holocaust survivor."

He rolled up his shirt to show Jerry the numbers.

7 . . . 4 . . . 1 . . . 7.

The last four digits of Jerry's social security number was 7416. And the memory of a conversation, held long ago but still very fresh and poignant, sprang to his mind: ". . . We were branded in numerical order . . . my parents, my sisters, my brothers, and I. I was next to last . . ." he recalled Yehuda Finerman telling him that summer day years before in the kibbutz.

Jerry's reverie was broken by the American's tortured sobs.

"I lost my whole family in the concentration camp!" he cried. "Everyone was killed except for me! I have no one in the world!"

Jerry stared at the American in shock, and gently, very gently, he whispered, "My dear friend . . . you are wrong. Number 7416 is very much alive. And I happen to know exactly where he can be found."

*Father* O'Reilly* was a busy man. As a hospital chaplain who ministered at four local hospitals, he was on call twenty-four hours a day, and he had witnessed a lot of pain, heartache, and misery during the course of his ten-year career. To replenish himself and seek respite from the grinding schedule that occasionally wore him down, he often retreated to an abandoned theological seminary building where he had studied in his youth. Here he engaged in prayer, meditated, read, or simply allowed his mind to wander, his muscles to relax. He always felt renewed after a visit to this building. It was deserted, crumbling, and in a state of disrepair, but for him it had become a true sanctuary.

Late one afternoon, after a particularly taxing and difficult day, Father O'Reilly decided that a visit to the seminary building was in order. He yearned for its quiet and tranquil air, and his soul urgently needed to withdraw. He craved a place where he could breathe, think, and dream . . . alone.

He entered the old building, which had been forsaken long ago, but whose doors remained open to the few pilgrims who still sought its solace. He inhaled its musty odor of abandonment and smiled in rueful recollection as he envisioned the hundreds of hurrying students who had raced down its corridors with such life, such vitality. "Everything changes," he thought.

Just then, his hospital pager went off.

"Oh, no," he sighed. "Just when I was beginning to unwind."

He tried to retrieve his message, but for some reason it was strangely garbled.

"That's odd," he thought. "What's the matter with the pager?" Someone had paged him, but he couldn't figure out whom. Which hospital needed him?

The old seminary building had no operating telephones, so he had to leave its grounds to make his calls to the four hospital chaplaincy departments that had his beeper number.

*No,* said everyone he called. *We didn't call you. Try the other hospitals.* He tried them all, but the staff in each hospital was as perplexed as he was. No one who had his pager number had given him a call.

"The pager must be malfunctioning," he mused, as he returned to the old seminary building to continue his disrupted retreat. "I'll have to bring it into the company tomorrow to be repaired," he thought as he entered the seminary grounds.

Then he stopped and stared in disbelief.

During his absence, a wing of the old building had collapsed onto itself.

The very wing in which he had stood . . . only minutes before.

$I$n 1966, best-selling author and pilot Richard Bach was barnstorming in the Midwest in a rare biplane, a 1929 Detroit-Parks P-2A Speedster.

Stopping over in Palmyra, Wisconsin, Bach lent the plane to a friend, who upended the craft as he came in for a landing at the small airport. Working together, they were able to successfully repair the damaged plane, except for one part. A strut had been shattered and needed to be replaced. Bach and his friend felt discouraged by what they agreed were the very dim prospects for finding a replacement strut in Palmyra. There were only seven other biplanes in the world like his, and what were the chances of someone in a small town like Palmyra possessing that particular part?

As Bach and his friend stood near the plane, lamenting the hopeless situation, a man walked up to them and asked if he could be of any help. Bach replied sarcastically, "Sure. Do you just happen to have an inter-wing strut for a 1929 Detroit-Parks Speedster, model P-2A?"

The man walked over to a hangar and moments later returned with precisely the part that was required to fix the plane!

In his book *Nothing by Chance*, Bach reflects:

"The odds against our breaking the biplane in a little town that happened to be home to a man with the 40-year-old part to repair it; the odds that he would be on the scene when the event happened; the odds that we'd pushed the plane right next to his hangar, within ten feet of the part we needed — the odds were so high that 'coincidence' was a foolish answer."

❧

### Comment
Every once in a while we are reminded to take a step back, look up and simply acknowledge the hand that guides our life.

*I thought* my marriage was idyllic. I thought my husband was a respectable, upright, law-abiding citizen. I thought we had an open, honest relationship in which we knew everything there was to know about each other.

But when I discovered the cache of drugs hidden in his briefcase one day, I realized that everything I had assumed about my husband and about our marriage was a total sham.

Fifteen years of pretense came crashing down around me as I examined the small plastic bags of cocaine powder stashed in the pouch compartment. How had the truth eluded me all this time? How could I have been so naive? How could I have lived with a hard-core addict and not even known?

It wasn't the shock of discovering that he was an addict that pulled me away from him irrevocably. I could have lived with the knowledge that my husband had a serious problem; I am a loyal person and I would have given him my support. Together, we could have attempted to surmount the crisis. But the realization that all these years he had *lied* to me, perpetrated constant deceptions, engaged in endless subterfuge in order to maintain his habit and hide it from me: that realization I simply could not countenance.

For me, honesty between partners was the paramount thing; without it there could be no relationship.

So, there I was, a newly-divorced forty-year-old, with five children on my hands, and no marketable skills. All my life, I had devoted myself to home and hearth, eschewing the lure of the workplace in order to be a constant presence in my children's lives. When I had left my job to have my first baby, no office boasted a computer system. Now, they all did. How was I going to support my family?

"Displaced homemaker" was the term they used for me and tens of thousands of women like me.

I sat in agency after agency, scribbling applications for training courses and emergency relief. I was assured that help would soon be on its way. But in the meantime, there were bills to pay and five young and hungry mouths to feed. How was I going to get by?

I baby-sat a little; I tried telemarketing at night. But until I was accepted into a training program and acquired real skills, every month would prove a tremendous challenge.

One day, I couldn't take it anymore. The strain and burden were too great to bear. The next month's rent was due the following day and I was $240 short. The refrigerator and cupboards were bare; I didn't know what I would serve my children for supper that night. Each month I had somehow managed to pay the rent and feed the kids. But now, I seemed to be at the end of my rope. Everything was unraveling. Including me.

I began to weep. I felt utterly alone and helpless. To whom could I turn?

*Pray!* a voice inside me urged.

*Pray?* another voice scoffed.

Why not? I shrugged. It certainly couldn't hurt.

Out of the depths of my being, I prayed. From my torment and anguish and heartache and pain, I prayed. I prayed as I had never prayed before.

"Dear God," I prayed. "Please help me pay this month's rent and feed my children tonight. I'm not asking you to give me luxuries or extravagances; I'm begging you to allow me to *survive.*"

Just then, there was a knock at the door, and my aunt and uncle burst into the room, bearing bags of groceries. I stared at them in shock.

I was taken by surprise not merely because my aunt and uncle lived in a different part of town, but because for years they had been somewhat estranged from our family and had kept in touch only sporadically. I had not spoken to either of them in months.

Yet here they were, only seconds after I had completed my prayers — flesh-and-blood answers to my supplications!

So frightened was I by the juxtaposition of their sudden and unexpected arrival with my prayers, that I could only stammer my surprise and gratitude.

After they left, I pondered — with awe and fear — the mystery of their auspicious visit. I had not spoken to anyone recently who was in contact with them, and I had been too proud to tell my friends and relatives the extent of my troubles. No one had known that my cupboards were empty.

When I had attempted to ask my aunt and uncle what had brought them to my home, they had casually answered, "Oh, we were just in the neighborhood, and thought you could use some extra stuff."

An unsatisfactory answer, indeed.

I was overwhelmed with relief knowing that my children would eat heartily that night. But what would I do about the rent?

As I began to unpack the groceries, I noticed a white envelope discreetly tucked into one of the bags. It had my name on it.

I tore it open and found inside twelve crisp $20 bills. $240.

Two hundred forty dollars is a strange amount of money to give as a gift.

But it was precisely the amount I needed for the rent.

—*Chrissie Jenkins* \*

꧁꧂

*Comment*

Set a prayer in motion and you've set a bird with a pointed beak soaring to the sky. Watch it, as it pierces the gates of heaven.

*I*n 1977, Teri Baucum was swimming in a lake with her young brothers and her dog when she stepped on something sharp. She bent down to retrieve it and found herself clutching a mud-encased, mollusk-encrusted class ring. Inside the band of the heavy, aristocratic-looking ring was an inscription: *"K. Sprott, 1956."*

"Geez," she said, and emitted a low whistle. "This thing's been here a long time."

Perhaps, had she been older, she would have thought of pursuing inquiries that would have led her to the college that issued the ring and, ultimately, to its owner. Or she might have launched her own personal investigation of the lakeside area, in an attempt to ferret out the owner's name. But she was a mere slip of a girl, young and unsophisticated, and she was ignorant of the myriad ways one could track down an owner's identity.

Since class rings aren't particularly valuable, anyhow, it never even occurred to her to embark on an extensive search. Still, she didn't feel it was quite right to simply toss the ring back into the water. "I'll hold onto it," she thought. "You never know."

So she took the ring home, threw it in a drawer, and promptly forgot about its existence. But every time she moved, she retrieved the ring that was tucked into a corner of her dresser drawer and took it along with her to her new home. "Why do I keep holding on to this old ring?" she asked herself every now and then, perplexed by her own actions. "What's the point?"

Twenty years and four states later, Teri was happily married and living on a lakefront property. Early one Saturday morning, her husband was standing on the outdoor patio, admiring the view, when his attention was captured by an unusual sight. He ran into the bedroom shouting, oblivious to the deep slumber in which his wife was enwrapped. "Hey, Ter, wake up and come see this!"

Teri pulled the covers up over her head. She didn't work on Saturdays as her husband did, and she wanted to revel in the luxury of a late morning in bed. But her husband was insistent, and finally, to oblige him, she groggily pulled herself out of bed and stumbled outside to see the cause of his excitement.

A large hot-air balloon was floating serenely over the lake. "Very nice, honey," she said dutifully, and made a beeline back to bed. "Hope I can get back to sleep," she thought wearily, unimpressed by the spectacle that had so enthralled her spouse.

But fifteen minutes later, her husband rushed into the bedroom again, his enthusiasm now changed to alarm.

"You gotta look at this balloon *now*," he yelled. "It seems like it's out of control. It's rushing over the lake and it's headed in our direction! This thing's gonna crash *right into our house!*

"Don't be ridiculous," Teri mumbled to her husband, pulling the covers up over her head once more.

But her sleep was interrupted a third time just a few minutes later by a furious pounding on the window. It was her husband, now gesticulating wildly. She dashed outside, galvanized by his frenzied behavior.

True to his dire prediction, the balloon had plummeted down from the sky onto their house!

The balloon was tangled up in the branches of the tree that shaded the house and in the wires from the television cable system, and the balloonist was hanging onto a rope for dear life. "Oh my God, he's going to die!" Teri thought in horror.

She watched helplessly as her husband carefully shimmied up the tree toward the balloon that was careening ominously over the side of their roof. Slowly, laboriously, he eased an older man and a young boy out of the basket in which they were trapped. Finally, after what seemed like an eternity, he had them successfully extricated and they were safe on the ground.

The older man brushed himself off and then gallantly extended his hand. "Thank you so much for saving our lives! My name is Kingswood Sprott Junior."

And without missing a beat, Teri replied:

"And I . . . I have your class ring!"

"*R*on, is that you?" came the frantic voice on the phone.

"Yes, what is it?" asked Ron, noting the concern in his sister's voice.

"It's Caron," came the reply . "She's sick, very sick, and she needs to go to the hospital! Meet us at Mount Sinai as soon as you can!"

Upset by the news, Ron turned to his secretary. "Carol, that was my sister. You remember my niece Caron Graham? Well, she needs to get to the hospital and I'm going to see if I can help in any way. Please cancel my afternoon appointments." Ron grabbed his coat from the closet and ran out.

When Carol got home from work she told her five-year-old son about Caron. He listened intently. He then went to his bedroom. A few minutes later he returned with a paper rose in his hand.

"Mom, could you get this rose to Caron?" he asked.

"Oh, honey," said Carol, obviously moved by her son's gesture. "I have such a busy day tomorrow. I'll try. Perhaps on my way to the office. Wherever did you find such a thing?"

"Last Sunday when we were at mass, Mom, I noticed this rose lying in the aisle beside our pew. When you went up for communion, I bent down to pick it up. That's when an old lady with a shawl wrapped around her, someone I had never seen before, came over to me and said that the rose was meant for someone who needed a miracle. And then she said, 'Be sure to put the rose into the person's hand so that it touches the skin.' I bet this rose was meant for Caron, Mom."

Carol looked adoringly at her son and took the rose. "I'll be sure to press it into Caron's hand. I promise. And, now, young man, how about some supper?"

The following morning Carol headed for Mount Sinai's intensive care unit, where she found several family members, including Ron, standing gravely around Caron's little bed. It was clear that Caron's condition was critical. The monitor perched on top of Caron's bed said it all. The reading was in the low sixties, perilously below the normal 100 mark.

Carol approached the bed. Gently she placed the paper rose in Caron's hand. Remembering her son's words, she made sure that the rose touched the frail girl's body.

She now waited. She had no illusions about any possible recovery. Nevertheless she closed her eyes and said her own silent prayer.

Almost at once she heard Caron's mother say excitedly: "Look, the number is rising!"

Carol immediately looked over at the monitor. Could her eyes be deceiving her?

Sure enough. The family members chimed in unison as the indicator started to climb: "64, 65, 66, 67, 68, 69."

The voices were now getting too loud for the intensive care unit. Alarmed, two nurses ran over to see what the commotion was about. The excitement around little Caron's bed was palpable. The figures continued to climb. They were now up to 95.

"Can you believe this!" Caron's mother cried.

"It's impossible," said Ron. The other family members shouted with joy the final five figures: "96, 97, 98, 99, 100!"

The rose had done its job. Color returned to Caron's face. No one seemed to understand what had happened. Carol, of course, did. Unobtrusively she released the little paper rose from Caron's grip and slipped it back into her purse.

All who were there in the intensive care unit—the staff, the doctors, the nurses, but most of all Caron's family—pause from time to time to remember what they saw that day. And to reflect with wonder and awe.

❦

### Comment

That which may seem to be mundane has the power to transform us in the most sublime way, for in truth, nothing in God's world is mundane.

*Douglas* Johnson of London, England, unaccountably took the wrong bus home one afternoon and did not realize it until he had traveled some distance. Instead of going back and getting his usual bus, Johnson decided to stay on the wrong bus and enjoy the scenery of a different ride.

The bus took him to an outlying district of London where he rarely went. The bus passed by the apartment building of a woman who had been a client two years before. Johnson impulsively decided to get off the bus and visit her, since he was in the area. He made his way to her apartment and knocked. There was no answer. Then he smelled gas. He knocked again and shouted. Still no answer. Johnson broke down the door and discovered the woman lying unconscious, her head in the oven, a suicide attempt.

Fortunately, Johnson was just in time to save her life.

—*Alan Vaughan*

### Comment

To appear in the right place at the right time is to be a participant in a cosmic plan.

"*I'm* headed for the bar tonight. Do you want to come?" said Michelle Holder to her friend Dawn Montgomery. Rambunctious and restless, Michelle knew she could always count on her wild friend Dawn to party with her. This night was no exception.

"I'm waiting for you," came Dawn's eager reply. Moments later, Michelle pulled her car up in front of Dawn's building. She was dressed and ready to go. Dawn slipped into the passenger seat and beamed at her friend. Both their boyfriends, Shaun and Doug, were sailors away on duty. That meant they had plenty of time to themselves, and they felt the freedom.

"The night is ours!" laughed Michelle as she put the car into drive and stepped on the gas. Out of sheer habit, Dawn tried to pull down her safety belt, only to be reminded that, of course, it was no use. Over the entire three years she had known Michelle, the passenger safety belt in Michelle's car had been broken. Completely. Not only did it refuse to extend more than a few inches, but it had no buckle, just a strap. As usual, Dawn just shrugged and said, "Fine, hit the road."

Dawn never minded that the seat belt was broken. In fact, it was kind of fun. She lived recklessly, on the edge, and liked to court danger. If she saw a patrolman pull up alongside the car, she would pull the safety belt over her shoulder. Once they were out of sight, she could throw the broken belt back with impunity. "Ha! Tricked them again!" was her attitude.

That night Michelle and Dawn hit their favorite hot spot: the Beach Club Bar in Oceanside, California. The music throbbed and the liquor flowed. Dancing and flirting, both women drank a few too many cocktails. By the end of the evening, when they emerged from the bar, they were drunk—sloppy drunk. "Oh, my goodness," Dawn slurred, "I can't even see where the car is."

"Isn't it that one over there?" muttered Michelle, stumbling as she pointed to the far corner of the parking lot. The two could hardly walk, but they held on to each other, giggling, and eventually shuffled to the car. Their laughter subsided once they climbed in the car, however. Michelle had a momentary flash of lucidity and turned serious. "I think we should just sleep in the car," she said, "since neither one of us can make out the steering wheel."

"Great idea," agreed Dawn, slumping over. The two passed out cold.

It could have been minutes, it could have been hours, but sometime later Dawn woke up feeling wind in her face. For a fraction of a second she felt alarmed. "Oh, no!" she thought. "Is Michelle actually driving this thing? Could we be on the freeway?" But the effects of the alcohol had not yet worn off, and Dawn found she was unable to sit up. She dismissed her thoughts as being part of a crazy dream, and fell back into a deep sleep. But indeed, Michelle did decide to drive in her drunken stupor.

The next thing Dawn remembers is waking up to the bright white glare of fluorescent lights. Her body was covered with bandages, and a snarl of catheters connected her to all sorts of machines. She was struck with terror. "Where am I?" she screamed.

A policeman standing nearby came to her bedside. "This is an emergency room," he said. "I'm afraid you and your friend have been in a terrible accident."

From across the room Dawn could hear Michelle's screams. "How is my friend?" Dawn demanded.

"She's bad," the policeman replied gravely. "They're pulling glass out of her face. Your car hit a pole on the bridge, and she came flying out the window. Her face hit the ground with all the shattered pieces of glass."

Dawn leaned back and closed her eyes. Could this really be happening? Or was it merely a bad dream, an extension of her drunken slumber? To some extent, the alcohol was still in her system. On top of that, she had been given codeine to minimize the pain. Her feelings were somewhat dulled, but nevertheless, she felt welling up in her a sharp anger at God. "Why did you let me survive?" she cried. "Why didn't you just let me die?"

Just then, the urgent words of the policeman interrupted her thoughts. "You guys could've been dead," he said.

But Dawn was not in the mood to talk. "I know," she replied flatly, hoping to end the conversation.

But the officer would not be deterred. "If it wasn't for your good sense, we might have had to call your parents to identify you," he said.

"My good sense?" Dawn fired back. "What do you mean?"

"Wearing that seat belt!" the policeman replied.

*"Seat belt?"* Dawn was mystified. She shouted at the officer that the seat belt in the car didn't even work, that it didn't even have a buckle. But the officer would not be fooled, not this time. "Look," he said, pointing to the report of the paramedics. "Right here they wrote that they had to cut your sweater and seat belt to get you out of the car. They did it just in time, since the car was hovering over the side of the bridge. As soon as they got you out, the car tipped over and went plunging down into the water below. But I tell you—if not for your seat belt, you would have gone right through the windshield, and down in the water, too."

Dawn Montgomery could hardly believe what she was hearing; then she looked down at her body and was even more amazed by what she saw. There, across her chest and below her waist, was a black and blue mark, in an unmistakable outline. The bruise was in the exact shape of a seat belt.

During her several weeks of recuperation, Dawn was perplexed by the mystery.

Dawn left the hospital and Michelle stayed behind, still recovering from her wounds. So when the day came for her father to come pick her up from the hospital, she asked him for a favor. "Dad," she said, "on the way to the house, I'd like to stop at the junkyard. I hear the car was found, and I know where it is, and I just need to check something out." Once in the car, Dawn's father realized that the junkyard was out of the way, but he was so grateful to have his daughter alive and well that he agreed to her request. "Sure," he said, "just point the way." At the junkyard, Dawn scanned the heaps of twisted metal until she recognized Michelle's car. The passenger window was open, and she managed to peer inside at that old, familiar seat belt. What she saw made her shiver. Without any doubt, there was now a hard metal buckle where once there had been only a frayed strap.

*Postscript:* After the accident, which occurred on April 19, Dawn vowed to become sober. She made several false starts until July 22, when she finally entered the recovery program she has attended ever since. Dawn considers the day she became sober the first day she really began her life.

But what about the miracle that saved her life that fateful night? Maybe she had a kindred spirit watching over her. Dawn's grandmother, Irene Kohen, died long before she was born. Yet the family has always been amazed at how Dawn—with her vivacious personality, fiery red hair, and warm blue eyes—is the spitting image of Irene. Indeed, family members say the resemblance is so striking, they believe Dawn just might be Irene's reincarnation.

What's more, the two women's lives seem to have intersected on two key dates. The day of Dawn's accident, April 19, was the exact day that Irene Kohen passed away. And the day that Dawn started life anew and became sober, July 22, was—ironically— the day of Irene Kohen's birthday.

ᥫᩣ

### Comment

When we are blessed with divine intervention, a life returned becomes a life joyfully reclaimed.

*I love* my work as television's "Frugal Gourmet," sharing my kitchen with viewers for half an hour each week. I'm glad I have been able to provide a comfortable life for my wife, Patty, and two sons, Channing and Jason. It's tempting sometimes to think that success is a by-product of my own hard work. But early in my career, when it seemed I had lost everything, I learned an important lesson about just who is really in charge.

Back when I was a young minister, I was the chaplain of the University of Puget Sound in Tacoma, Washington. I taught a course on first-century worship. One day a young woman gave a report on a book that discusses food and theology. This so caught the imagination of my students and me that we designed a new course called Food as Sacrament and Celebration, which also included daily lunch. The course was so popular it filled up every semester long before registration was officially opened.

I enjoyed working with food so much I soon opened a catering service with some of my students. It meant putting in long, hard hours, but I had always had workaholic tendencies. And since my wife and I had just bought our first house and wanted to start a family, it seemed to make sense to branch out. Finally, I left my job at the university to run a cooking school and open a cookware store. Since I'm an "in control" kind of guy, I had my hands in everything.

Then in 1973 a producer friend called and asked if I would do something for the local PBS station in Tacoma. I used to say the station was so small that it had a broadcast radius of six blocks. But this guy was a friend and he needed a favor, so once a week I brought all my own food, pots, pans and helpers over and we did a cooking show.

My students and I also printed our own cookbooks, which I stored in piles in my basement. With the school, the store and the shows, I believed God had given me a wonderful and unusual venue for ministry, reaching people I would never get to meet in a church setting. But often I felt frantic to keep up, to keep tabs on every detail of each project.

After several exhausting years the television program became so successful that the large PBS station in Chicago decided to produce a series for national syndication, with the promise of continuing it on a regular basis if all went well. I flew to Chicago to shoot several segments, and things went so smoothly we set a starting date for the next season. It was a good thing, because as far as my business was concerned, everything else was falling apart. Suddenly there seemed to be a cooking school and kitchen shop on every corner. We had been losing money for a while when I finally sold out in early 1982.

One day, after letting the business go, I sat down with a stack of bills and determinedly paid them in the order they came up. The money was soon gone, but there were still bills left to pay. Big ones. After all my hard work I was short $70,000.

Thank God for Chicago, I thought. In only two weeks I would have an income again. I would be back on the treadmill, rushing to keep up, to stay in control. . . .

All along my wife had been trying to get me to slow down. "Think of your heart, Jeff," she warned.

It was a prudent warning. When I was a kid, I had rheumatic fever and had appeared to have made a full recovery. It wasn't till I was 15 that I had my first real physical. My doctor asked, "How long have you had this heart murmur?"

He sent me to a specialist, who said I would have to have the damaged valve replaced one day. But valve replacement surgery was just being developed. Doctors advised me to wait. So I repressed the fact that I had a time bomb in my chest, and got on with daily life.

Then came the summer of 1982. For months I had been tiring easily, but I attributed it to stress. The week before I was to fly to Chicago, I woke up in the morning straining for breath. "Patty," I gasped to my wife. "I'd better get to the doctor."

When I walked into my doctor's office, he took one look at me and told his secretary to call Dr. Lester Sauvage, a well known Seattle heart surgeon. Dr. Sauvage ran tests and immediately scheduled open-heart surgery—for the day I was supposed to tape my first show in Chicago. Patty called the producers and told them I wouldn't be able to make it.

Dr. Sauvage was honest about the prognosis. There were three possible outcomes: The operation would be a success; it would fail and I would die; or the trauma would send me into a permanent vegetative state.

I'll never forget the night before the surgery. I lay alone in the room, pondering my life. I had tried so hard to control everything. I had worked around the clock. I had driven myself till I was miserable, and where had it gotten me?

I was 42 years old, with no job, a family to support and seventy thousand dollars in debt. Because of my faith, I wasn't afraid of dying, but the prospect of becoming a vegetable was horrifying to me.

And there wasn't a thing I could do about any of it.

It was then I remembered reading what theologian Rudolf Bultmann said about being pushed up against the wall: When you're so frightened you don't know what to do, you finally either know death or you know grace. And grace, to paraphrase Bultmann, is when you're up against the wall and you suddenly realize you're not in control of things — and that's okay.

My life was in God's hands; it had always been in God's hands. I had just acted as if it were in mine, as if everything were up to me. The word I got during that dark night was simply this: Trust the Holy One and relax.

"Lord," I said, "my life is yours. My health is yours. My debt is yours. Teach me to relax."

The next morning this message was again brought home to me. As I looked up at Dr. Sauvage in the operating room, I knew with absolute finality that control of my life was totally out of my hands.

When I woke up after surgery, my first thought was, *I can think!* This was the greatest joy I had known. I began a prayer of thanksgiving.

As I recuperated, I also felt a surge of spiritual energy. God had given me my life; I had given him my future. Every time I started to worry about my $70,000 debt, or my bleak job prospects, I wrested control from myself and gave it back to the Holy One.

The TV producers in Chicago called to find out how I was, and promised my wife they would keep in touch, but I didn't count on it. The old Jeff would have been in knots, but now I knew it was in God's hands, not mine. Then I got an unexpected invitation to be on Phil Donahue's show.

For luck, I took along copies of that old spiral-bound cookbook. "How much should we say they sell for?" Phil asked when I got there. Each book had cost me three dollars to produce, so I had been selling them for $4.75.

Three times, right before a commercial, Phil held up the cookbook, and a placard on the screen told people where to write. "This is the man! This is the book!" he shouted happily.

After the show, one of the producers said to me as I was leaving, "I hope you have a lot of books."

"And how," I said glumly. "I've got five thousand of them sitting in my basement."

I'll never forget the look of disbelief she gave me. "Five thousand?" she repeated. "You're in real trouble!"

It turned out I was. Orders started pouring in—and didn't stop! In those days, syndicated shows were shipped around the country from station to station. It took about nine weeks for a particular Phil Donahue show to air on all the stations, and I had to keep printing more and more books. At the end of those nine weeks, I had sold 40,000 cookbooks.

Not long after that, my phone rang in Tacoma, and it was Frank Lieberman from PBS in Chicago. "All right, Smith, quit fooling around," he roared in mock annoyance. "We know you've recovered. When are you coming to start a new TV series?"

I couldn't wait to get going again. Not because I was frantic to control every facet of my life, but because I wanted to work. I would work hard, but this time I would work hard out of devotion to God, not because I was driven to call all the shots.

For God in his mercy had truly shown me he could meet my needs. *You* do the math: Multiply those 40,000 books I sold times $1.75 profit, and how much do you get? *Seventy thousand dollars exactly.*

And a heaping serving of grace.

—*Jeff Smith*

*W*hen it came to love,
Mary Margaret Dereu
was blessed. For thirty-four wonderful years, she was
married to her soul mate, Eugene. She had many pet
names for him, but mostly she called him her "Prince."

Then, on October 24, 1995, Eugene unexpectedly
passed away in his sleep. Mary was devastated. They were
just three months shy of their thirty-fifth anniversary.

Days turned into weeks, which turned into months,
and with the passing of time, a slow healing took place.
But as Valentine's Day of the following year came
around, Mary found herself inconsolable about
Eugene's death. To distract herself, she took a drive
downtown, ready to lose herself in the sights and sounds
of the local market.

Once inside the market, Mary glanced at several
booths, but nothing in particular caught her eye. Then,
suddenly, she found herself beckoned by a row of
camellia bushes in the corner of the marketplace. The
flowers were majestic, in full bloom, pure white. They
reminded her of the flowers at her wedding, and she
purchased a bush without any hesitation.

At home, Mary chose a special place beside Eugene's
favorite shade tree to plant her new shrub. While she
covered the roots with earth, she kept repeating "Happy
Valentine's Day, Eugene . . . Happy Valentine's Day,
my Prince."

Then, just as she leaned on one hand to stand up, a small white tag attached to the base of the plant happened to catch her eye. She might easily have overlooked it.

"They must name these bushes just as they name rosebushes," Mary thought. She turned the tag in her muddy fingers. She read the name and felt the sting of a tear. There, in black ink, was the name of the pure white flower: Prince Eugene.

Perhaps it was his kiss, blown from beyond.

### Comment

Flowers are often the messengers of our emotions, hopes, and dreams. Through them we send and receive, in this world and beyond.

*N*ineteen-year-old Chris Graham and twenty-year-old Steve Ashton were on their way from Manhattan to an upstate New York park that boasted superior recreational grounds and a large scenic lake. They had arranged to meet several friends at a specific site near the lake at exactly 1 P.M. and they looked forward to a day of boating, fishing, swimming, and more.

But all day long, as they traveled the New York State Thruway, they found themselves plagued by an unusual series of mishaps, crises, and problems, and it seemed to them as if they would never get there.

First, a flat tire. They pulled onto a shoulder of the highway and changed it quickly. "Not too bad," Chris muttered. "Only fifteen minutes gone. We'll still get there in time."

Then, after making a quick stop at a Thruway rest area, they turned the key in the ignition of the car and nothing happened. Several red signs began flashing a warning on the dashboard control panel, and Steve, who was driving, sighed. "I'm afraid the battery's dead. Gotta find someone with cables; I don't have any myself." It took about half an hour to find someone else who did.

When the battery was recharged, they sped down the highway to make up for lost time. "There are never any cops on the Thruway," Steve reassured Chris, who was nervous. "They all stalk Route 17 instead."

They were pulled over by a sheriff who didn't seem aware of this ironclad rule.

He took a *very* long time to write the ticket.

"We're an hour late already!" expostulated Chris. "The guys will never wait for us, and we'll never be able to find them. The park's huge."

"Relax," soothed Steve. "We're not so far away. I just gotta find the next exit and get off the highway here, according to the directions Johnny gave me. The rest of the way is small country roads. Maybe we'll have better luck on them than the Thruway."

But just as they pulled off at the exit, the car suddenly sputtered and died.

The two looked at each other.

"Now what?" cried Chris.

"Is this for real?" Steve shook his head in disbelief.

It took an hour for the tow truck to arrive.

"Remind me to call the customer relations department of AAA tomorrow and give them a piece of my mind," Steve said crossly.

"It's the fan belt," the mechanic at the shop said. "It'll take at least two hours."

"I give up!" shrieked Chris. "Can you believe our bad luck? When the car's fixed, let's head back home."

"I'm not a quitter," Steve said stubbornly. "The park's only about twenty minutes away from here. I don't want to turn around at this point. We're almost there. Let's go to the park and see if we can find the guys. We still have a couple of hours of sunlight left. I bet we'll find the guys after all; you'll see," Steve promised Chris in an optimistic voice.

But when they finally arrived four hours late at the appointed meeting site near the lake, the place was deserted.

"I just can't believe our day," Chris grumbled to Steve. "We came all this way for nothing!"

*"Help!"* they suddenly heard a young voice shout.

*"Help us, please!"* a second voice cried.

For a frozen moment, Chris and Steve were motionless, their gaze riveted on the sight of two little boys flailing in the lake. Then the two—certified lifeguards both—raced to the water's edge and dove in. They pulled out the kids, administered CPR, and saved their lives.

Afterwards, a shaken Steve turned to Chris and asked in a trembling voice, "Do you understand what went down here, Chris?"

"I do, Steve," Chris answered somberly. "I most certainly do."

"If we hadn't gotten to the park at precisely the time we did, surely those kids would be dead."

## Comment

It's a mistake to believe that "coincidences" happen only for *our* sakes. Sometimes, they happen *to* us, but they may not be happening *because* of us or *for* us. What seems to be happening to us is actually occurring for the sake of another. It's not really *our* script, even though we may be major players. When a coincidence occurs that makes no sense in how it impacted our lives, we must also ask: But did it impact someone else's?

*I rarely* allow myself the luxury of a taxi, but on this particular day in September 1997 I found myself suddenly caught in a torrential downpour in midtown Manhattan, lacking an umbrella or a raincoat and on my way to an important job interview. It wouldn't impress anyone, I thought glumly, if I arrived in a rain-splattered suit and had a sopping mass of tangled curls. "Drenched" does not translate into "dresses well," a definite requisite for any job candidate these days. So I hailed a cab and hopped in.

I saw the bracelet immediately. Its gold veneer glinted at me and I lifted it from the corner of the passenger seat where it rested. It was studded with diamonds, and although I am neither a connoisseur nor an expert, I knew they were real. This was an expensive piece of jewelry, I thought, the kind of jewelry I myself longed for but could probably never hope to own. Out of my league completely, or at least for the next decade, I sighed, envisioning the lean years that lay ahead until my young husband and I established ourselves financially.

I examined the bracelet closely and saw that its clasp was broken. "The woman passenger before me must have lost it just as she left the taxi," I thought. "She probably didn't even realize it was gone."

"Hey, look at this! . . ." I began to shout excitedly to the taxi driver, then suddenly reconsidered, mid-sentence.

"Whaddja say?" he asked, turning around to stare at me through the bulletproof partition.

"Look at this . . . rain!" I dissembled. "Isn't it unbelievable!"

"If I show him the bracelet, he'll just pocket it himself," I thought. "Why does he deserve it more than me? I'm the one who found it! Besides, Judy's brother's engagement party is coming up Saturday night. Her mother's always dripping with jewels and looking so classy. For once, I'd like her to see me looking classy, too. This bracelet would really impress her."

So I pocketed the bracelet and didn't breathe a word to the cabbie.

In truth, I had absolutely no qualms about what I had done. There are over seven million people living in the metropolitan New York area, and at least 20,000 cabs. Even if I tried to find the owner, given the odds, the chances were slim.

But back in Brooklyn my mother's equanimity was shaken, shaken badly, when I recounted to her the tale of my triumphant find.

"I'm shocked," she said, her voice cold. "Shocked and very disappointed. I thought I imbued my children with a sense of honesty and integrity. How could you have taken it?"

"If I had given it to the cabbie, he would just have taken it for himself," I argued. "What should I have done?"

"You *should* have brought it to the taxi company that owns the fleet of cabs. Or the Taxi and Limousine Commission. I'm sure they have a lost and found department. Not only *should* you have done this, you *will* do this," said my mother, her voice now steel. *"Today!"*

"Geez, Mom," I expostulated, "I really wanted to wear the bracelet to Judy's brother's engagement party Saturday night. It wouldn't do any harm if I keep it until then."

*"Today,"* my mother commanded.

Saturday night, I entered the catering hall in Queens with trepidation. "Everyone in Judy's family dresses so fancy," I thought crossly. "If only I had that gold and diamond bracelet, I would feel more chic."

I latched onto the line of well-wishers filing past the family, and when I reached Judy, her brother, and his fiancée Sandy, I gave them each a hug and a kiss. I felt more distant toward Judy's mother, though, and, refraining from my usual more effusive displays of affection, reached to shake her hand. Regal and aristocratic, she extended her hand to me graciously, and I clasped it firmly.

It was then that I saw it. The bracelet. Her tiny-boned wrist was encircled by the same gold and diamond bracelet I had found in the cab earlier that week in Manhattan. Could it be? Was it possible? Maybe it was a replica? Maybe the designer had made dozens? It couldn't be the *same* bracelet I had found, could it? It was just a coincidence, right?

But when I later took Judy aside and gushed convincingly about the "gorgeous bracelet your mother is wearing," Judy told me proudly: "It's a one-of-a-kind creation. My mother's friend, a famous jewelry designer, designed it especially for her. It's my mother's favorite piece. She lost it earlier this week, in a cab, and was utterly devastated. She thought she would never get it back. Thank God, an honest citizen found it and brought it into the Taxi and Limousine Commission. She was so relieved. She would have felt terrible if she had not been able to wear it tonight."

—*Sally Larson*

### Comment

Attempts to hide the truth are futile, for truth, like oil in water, will always rise to the surface.

*W*hen the phone rang, Debby picked it up, not expecting anything out of the ordinary. But when she heard the voice on the other end of the line, she froze in shock. It was the hospital, with the kind of news that is every mother's worst nightmare.

"Your son's been in a car accident—get here as soon as you can," said the official on the other end of the line, before elaborating on the grisly specifics.

Though Debby could hardly speak, she did manage to say, "I'll be there in fifteen minutes."

"Hurry," came the ominous response. "Come sooner if you can."

Debby hung up the phone and ran to her car. All the way to the hospital, she fretted and tried not to imagine the worst. But when she got there, she found her dear son of sixteen, Dan, in critical condition and near death. In fact, he registered 6 on the trauma scale, which is the point at which the hospital calls a coroner.

She wanted to throw her arms around him, but she could not, because there were tubes everywhere. Bending down to her son, she choked out, "Dan, Dan, can you hear me?"

The doctor came to her side. "Your son is in a coma," he gently told her. "He cannot hear you."

Debby was beside herself. The full reality of the situation came crashing down on her, and she broke into sobs. Not long ago, Debby's husband had passed away, and the thought that she might now lose her only son was unbearable. "This can't be happening," she cried.

But it was happening, and it only got worse. For the next few hours, Dan lay perfectly still, eyes shut, a far cry from the laughter-filled kid that he had been. To make matters worse, the doctors had no prognosis with which to quell Debby's fears. "It's still too early to tell" was the only medical report they could give her.

And thus the horrible hours went by. The hours turned into days and the days turned into weeks, but Dan remained in a coma. Seven weeks later, when he was deemed medically stable, he was transferred to a rehab hospital.

Meanwhile, Debby herself lived her life as if in a trance. When she wasn't working, she came to the hospital to sit by her son. Often she read to him, hoping that the sound of her voice would reach him somewhere, somehow. She kept a constant vigil for any signs of life, but his only response continued to be a slow, steady breathing.

And then, one Thursday night just before nine o'clock as she sat at Dan's bedside, Debby was struck with an idea. She was closing her book when she realized it was time for *Seinfeld* on television. For years, the *Seinfeld* show had provided Debby's family with laughter and an occasion to gather in the den. The memory of these evenings made Debby feel warm for the first time in weeks. The dog needed feeding, and she needed sleep, but this night, instead of heading for home,

Debby decided to tune in. "It will do me good to watch the show," she thought. "And it will be good for Dan too—after all, *Seinfeld* is his favorite show."

As the opening credits rolled, Debby settled into her chair. The familiar music drew her in, and the plot began to unfold. Then, as she turned to make herself more comfortable, she glanced at Dan and caught sight of his expression. His eyes had flown wide open. "Oh, my goodness!" she cried. In her amazement, she lurched from her seat, thinking the volume might be too loud. But his eyes remained open wide, confounding the nurse who came in to change his IV. Still, the show ended, and he didn't speak. It came time to leave. "Honey," she said, leaning over to say her good-byes for the night, "I'm going home. I've got to feed the dog. She's been in all day." She was in the process of straightening up when suddenly Dan's eyes began to flutter. "Where am I?" he managed to say. He was coming out of his coma.

Then it hit Debby in a flash. He had been watching his favorite show, and the familiar music and voices had reached him.

And yet, there is an ironic twist to this story. The *Seinfeld* show that night was actually about comas. Much to Debby's disbelief, the episode had centered on Kramer, who rented a video about a young woman in a coma—the result of an accident. Who could have known that tuning in that evening would reach Dan's slumbering mind and, in the end, help guide him back to life and laughter?

*S*ince I had invited two couples for dinner, I made yeast rolls in the morning and set them aside to rise. After I dusted, I kneaded the rolls down again and left them to rise once more.

The rolls were no sooner in the oven when two delivery men arrived with my new bookcase. They patiently moved the heavy bookcase to another wall space when it didn't look right in my first choice.

Following the men to the front door to thank them, I remembered my rolls.

"Wait a minute," I told them. "You worked so hard, I want to give you something." I covered the rolls with waxed paper and handed them over. "You can have these with your lunch."

I made another batch. When I kneaded them for their second rising, they looked every bit as good as the first batch. The doorbell rang again. It was my decorator, who had come to put up my needlepoint cornice board. When he finished, it looked so pretty with the new bookcase.

The decorator asked, "Do I smell homemade bread?" Handing over the waxed paper bundle with a smile, I thought, "Well, I still have plenty of time to make a third batch.

At about four that afternoon, a car pulled into my driveway. A friend dashed into the kitchen.

"I found these tomatoes on sale and thought you'd like some for your company tonight," she said.

Then she smelled the rolls I had just taken from the oven. "Oh, my husband thinks your rolls are better than anything in the world!"

Reaching for the waxed paper once again, I said, "Take these to him."

"But don't you need the rolls for your guests?" she asked.

"Don't worry," I reassured her.

After she left, I reasoned, "I guess tomatoes are healthier then rolls." It was too late to make more anyway.

When my guests arrived, Marge, first in the doorway, said: "I have a surprise for you!"

She handed me a fragrant loaf of bread, still warm from her oven.

One day I'll learn. You just can't outgive the lord.

*—Faye Field*

*Rabbinical* students at one of the most demanding and renowned theological seminaries in Israel lead an austere and Spartan life. They rise at 6 A.M. for morning prayers followed by a rigorous eighteen-hour day of exacting Talmudic studies. Except for mealtimes, their only real break comes in the late afternoon when they are allotted time off for the chores that typically consume young men living on their own for the first time in their lives.

During one such break, a throng of students had seized the opportunity to convene outside the seminary walls to enjoy the crisp autumn day. The air was brisk and invigorating, and after a muggy summer of steaming sidewalks and torpid temperatures, they welcomed the bracing chill in the air. They stood relaxed, chatting amiably, discussing the day's studies (some complex Talmudic passages that had confounded many), a few surreptitiously smoking cigarettes. The atmosphere was calm and pleasant. Absorbed by conversation and camaraderie, few paid heed to the action unfolding on the street.

The interest of one sharp-eyed young man, however, was piqued by a speck growing in the distance, and, stiffening, he motioned to his friends.

"Look at that!" he said, jabbing his finger at the spot rapidly advancing towards their street.

"How sad!" murmured several of his comrades, transfixed, as they absorbed the scene and assimilated its implications.

One lone Jewish hearse, unaccompanied by the customary long procession of mourners, with no entourage whatsoever and without a single escort in attendance, was moving slowly down their street.

The young men were riveted by the solitariness of that single hearse; it evoked a profound sense of pathos within them. How could someone go to his death so completely alone? Where were the family, the neighbors, the friends? Was it possible that the deceased had lived a life so detached and apart from the community that no one even knew—or cared—that he or she was dead?

They huddled together in silence, overcome by the dismal and melancholy scene. Their experience of the Jewish community was one of friendship, solidarity, unity, and support. They had never before witnessed such a stark demonstration of the lonely life that could be lived within it.

"This is just heartbreaking," one young man whispered.

"To be buried this way is a terrible thing," said a second.

"We've got to do something," urged another.

"Let's do what clearly has to be done," said a fourth. "Let's follow the hearse to the cemetery and participate in the burial."

"But not just *us*," exhorted another. "Let's run into the building quick and get *all* the guys to come!"

And they did.

Soon the hearse was escorted by a long and impressive cortege of hundreds of students, who followed it to the Jewish cemetery on the outskirts of town. It was only when they reached the gravesite and a rabbi—the sole occupant—emerged from the hearse, that they learned the identity of the deceased.

"Well, this is very fitting!" the rabbi exclaimed, when he asked who they were and from what yeshiva (seminary) they had come. "How did you learn about her death? No one even knew she existed anymore! She was such an eccentric, and she lived the life of a hermit for the last fifty years, rebuffing everyone's efforts to reach out to her. I'm shocked that anyone was even aware that she had died . . ."

The young men looked at him strangely, puzzled by his assumption. "Excuse me, rabbi," one said quietly. "We don't know the deceased. We don't know whom you're talking about."

Now it was the rabbi's turn to look discomfited. "You don't know whose funeral you're attending?" he asked in shock. "Then how and why are you here?"

The young men explained how affected they had been by the sight of the solitary hearse and how they had been moved to escort the deceased. How they had wanted to perform—purely and for its own sake—a *mitzvah,* a good deed.

After listening to the young men's earnest explanations, the rabbi began to cry.

"My dear friends," he said softly, "your presence here was clearly ordained. Seventy years ago, a wealthy Jewish businessman donated an expensive piece of real estate to the Jewish community for the purpose of building a rabbinical seminary. *Your* rabbinical seminary.

"Beyond the initial donation of the land and the building, during his lifetime the businessman continued to support the fledgling seminary with large sums of money that helped it flourish and become one of the premier institutions of its day.

"As he got older, the yeshiva, in recognition of his outstanding philanthropy, wished to bestow special honors and awards on him, but he was a humble man and he shunned them all.

"He had only one child—a daughter—whom he loved excessively. When rabbis would approach him and ask, 'How can we repay you for your unbelievable charity?' he would smile good-naturedly and say, 'Thank God, I am a rich and happy man; I don't need anything. But maybe one day, you can be of service to my beloved daughter. Maybe one day, she'll need your help.'

"The rabbis gave the philanthropist their solemn oath that the yeshiva would not forsake his daughter.

"After a long and productive life, he died, and sad to say, his daughter abandoned the religious traditions of her youth. She disconnected herself from the Jewish community, and was in and out of psychiatric institutions all her life.

"The rabbis who remembered their promise to her father tried repeatedly to keep in contact with her and lend her their support. But she rebuffed their overtures and lived a hermitlike, eccentric existence. Soon, the original group of rabbis who had made that pledge to her father died, and the pledge was forgotten. The daughter was abandoned and lived the sad and misbegotten life of a recluse.

"But, my friends, it is to *her* funeral that you've coincidentally come today, the funeral of the daughter of the benefactor of your very own yeshiva. With your presence here today, you have both fulfilled your rabbis' pledge and repaid the benefactor's largesse, once and for all."

Later, the rabbinical students learned that the hearse was not supposed to drive down their small, obscure street, blocks away from the main thoroughfare.

The driver had gotten lost, and had driven down their street by mistake.

*T*hroughout her forty-year marriage, Kelly O'Brien* had been a long-suffering, forbearing wife. Her husband, Chris, was the quintessential "Type A" personality—an aggressive, driven man and a veritable workaholic, whose ambition and energy had propelled him to the top of his field. Kelly, a mild-mannered, gentle woman with modest dreams, had stood discreetly on the sidelines while Chris determinedly pursued and fulfilled his goals.

She had been so patient. It seemed as if she was always waiting for Chris: She had waited up for him countless late nights keeping his dinner warm, long past the hour when he had originally been due home. She had waited in front of Broadway theaters and elegant restaurants, glancing ruefully at her wristwatch as appointed meeting times with Chris came and went with impunity. And she had waited for scheduled vacations, which she planned eagerly, to materialize, but they never did. At the last moment, Chris would invariably beg off, citing a "crisis at work," a "last-minute snafu," or an "unbelievable opportunity" that had to be "seized immediately."

"When are we finally going to live?" Kelly would gently chide.

"When I retire, honey," Chris vowed solemnly. "And I *will* ask for early retirement, I promise."

So Kelly waited patiently for her life with Chris to finally begin. "Just another six months," she whispered to herself, "before he turns sixty-two and retires. Then . . . we'll really start to live!" And she began to call travel agencies, avidly collecting brochures and travel guides and letting her imagination wander down paths she had avoided before.

But the free and idyllic existence Kelly yearned for was not meant to be.

Chris came home one day with a guilty look on his face mixed with ill-concealed excitement. "The company is starting up a new branch in Houston," he announced, "and they want me to head it. They'll pay for all the relocation expenses and double my salary. What do you say?" He looked pleadingly at his wife.

"Chris . . . you promised early retirement!" she said, astonished by the sudden turn of events.

"Ohgawd, Kelly, I can't retire! I love what I'm doing. I can't see myself playing golf or bridge, or even playing tourist. It was unrealistic of me to promise early retirement. I'll go nuts!"

Kelly saw her dreams dissolve into the vortex of her husband's dynamism, a dynamism so strong that once it was unleashed it carried her along on its powerful current. She could be unwilling with Chris but never unyielding. Once again, her own needs would have to be sacrificed on the altar of his ambitions.

"But . . . Houston," she objected feebly. "All my friends are *here*. The only person I know in Houston is your third cousin Katherine, whom I haven't talked to in ages. I'm too old to start over."

"Honey, look at it as an adventure!" he wheedled. "And I'll try my best to get us an apartment right near Katherine so you won't be lonely."

But the apartment he ultimately found proved to be on the other side of town.

"So sorry, hon," he apologized, embarrassed by his inability to make good on at least one promise. "But apparently, all the apartment complexes are clustered together in a newer section. Where Katherine lives there are only big houses, no rentals. I know you don't want to undertake all the work and headache that a house entails.

"Anyway," he continued more confidently, "you'll love the apartment complex. It has a pool and a spa and all kinds of classes. I'm sure you'll meet lots of new people right away!"

But she didn't. Most of the residents of the apartment complex were yuppies in their thirties and forties, away all day at work. Kelly felt lonely and isolated. She had called Chris's cousin Katherine a couple of times, but they hadn't been able to get together. "Soon," Katherine promised vaguely, underscoring Kelly's anxiety. It seemed that the promises made to her lately had all been insincere and had all been broken.

"When," she thought sadly, "will Chris finally keep one single promise he's made to me? Will he ever consider *my* needs?"

She brooded over these questions constantly, much as she tried to banish them from her mind.

"I'm turning into a cranky old hag!" she scolded herself. "Better do something constructive, keep my mind off my problems. I know what I'll do!" she thought, brightening a little. "I'll whip up a homemade cake for his birthday tonight and we'll celebrate. I haven't baked in years. Won't he be surprised!"

All day long, Kelly puttered happily in her kitchen, blending, stirring, whisking ingredients until she had produced a lovely cake that satisfied her own impeccable standards and made her proud. "Chris will love this," she thought. "He'll be so surprised to receive a cake."

She had planned the surprise with such girlish excitement, she couldn't help but be disappointed when Chris came home from work that night, carrying a big box containing . . . a birthday cake!

"Who gave it to you?" she asked, downcast that someone else had stolen her surprise.

"Oh, the guys at work thought I'd feel lonely having a birthday in a new place, so they chipped in and bought me this. Wasn't that nice?"

"Well, guess what?" she said cheerfully, trying to hide her chagrin. "Now you have *two*!" And she held aloft her famous Hawaiian Delight cake that had been his favorite years ago, and placed it in front of him.

"Mmm!" he murmured in delicious anticipation. "My all-time favorite! I remember how complicated this particular cake is to produce. It must have taken you hours. This is really a treat! Who can compare a bakery cake to a homemade one, especially one made by you! And, honey," he added, darting her a thoughtful look, "I promise that when *your birthday* comes up in a few months, you will also have *two* birthday cakes!"

The two laughed and giggled and chattered together like a pair of teenagers. "Maybe it's not the start of the new life I envisioned," Kelly mused to herself, "but maybe it won't be so bad, after all. It's not so hard to be in a strange town when the man you love is right there with you."

That night, Chris woke up with severe chest pains and called out to Kelly. Before she could reach for the phone to call the police, she heard a strangulated choking sound from his throat, and he was gone. Chris was dead.

"Come back to New York!" her friends and relatives urged Kelly after the funeral. "There's nothing there for you." But she was too depressed, too paralyzed by shock, to move. She had no energy, no will, to make the calls and take the necessary steps to facilitate her return. Just the thought of calling the utility companies to close her accounts made her weak.

"I will come back," she promised, "but I can't right now. Too many things to do."

But Kelly couldn't muster enough strength to do even one chore. "Tomorrow I'll get out of bed . . ." she promised herself. "It's too hot outside to go anywhere, anyway."

"Tomorrow" stretched into an interminable expanse of yesterdays, and Kelly's depression deepened. She felt forsaken and desolate, her loneliness heightened by the knowledge that it was in fact her sixtieth birthday and she was marking it . . . alone.

Kelly was sitting at her kitchen table in her terry-cloth robe, sipping a cup of coffee, when the doorbell rang. Standing at the threshold was Chris's cousin Katherine, holding aloft a large box.

"Open it," she urged.

Inside was a homemade birthday cake.

"B-but how did you know?" Kelly asked in astonishment.

"Kelly, I swear to God, I had the strangest dream last night. Chris came to me in the dream and said: 'Tomorrow is Kelly's birthday. I want you to make her a cake.' Who am I to argue with Chris?" Katherine joked. "So . . . happy birthday!"

A few minutes later, the doorbell rang again and a stranger was standing outside, also bearing a cake box.

"Mrs. O'Brien?" the elderly woman inquired sweetly. "I'm your next-door neighbor, Mrs. Thomas. May I come in? I feel so badly that all this time has passed and I never came round to introduce myself to you. Please excuse my terrible manners, but just at about the time that you first moved in, I was having some surgery and not feeling quite well. Then I heard your husband died — I'm so sorry — and I didn't want to impose upon your privacy or your grief. . . . Well, just today, I was in the bakery and was drawn to a cake in the showcase that said 'Happy Birthday!' Well, I know this sounds downright fanciful, but it seemed to be beckoning to me. And beyond any reason or logic, an inner voice deep inside of me said, 'Bring this cake to Mrs. O'Brien.' Well, I've lived long enough to know to obey my inner voice, so I hope you won't mind a foolish old woman's actions. . . . Now, it isn't by any chance your birthday today, is it?"

***

### Comment

A patient heart is a fertile field for life's sweetest miracles.

*W*hen my first child was born, I was living in Newton, Massachusetts, and I knew very few people there. I did not own a car; and the few married friends I had made in the neighborhood did not yet have babies. They were not involved in domestic life the way I became as soon as my baby was born.

Prior to my marriage, I had worked first as a teacher and later as a journalist for the *Boston Traveler*. But the year was 1947, and at that time it was customary, virtually the rule, for women to stay home with their children. So I found myself confined to my home practically all day long, and feeling very lonely. Truthfully, I was also very bored. My baby was my only companion and I felt my isolation keenly.

When my second child was born three years later, I vowed to make a different kind of life for myself. I was desperate to add a new and different dimension to my painfully solitary existence. So I hired a young woman to come in every day, and I taught her how to take care of the baby and my older son in my absence. She was very competent and I felt satisfied that I had prepared the way for my own separate life in addition to my life as a wife and a mother. There was only one minor problem: I didn't know what that "separate life" looked like or was going to be. Now that all the pieces were in place, I had absolutely no idea what to do next! I was ready for activity and involvement, but I didn't know what kind. Nonetheless, I was filled with yearning and hope. I waited with growing excitement for my destiny to unfold.

One day the telephone rang, and I heard a young woman's voice say: "Hello, I'm calling to invite you to join Hadassah."

I had been reading about the attempts to form the Zionist State, which was not yet the State of Israel, and I was very sympathetic to the cause. So, without pause or hesitation, I immediately said: "I would like to!"

The young woman on the other end of the line must have been quite surprised by my enthusiasm because she quickly responded: "And would you like to participate in our Membership Committee?" (I guess she wanted to make certain that I would become involved!) Again, I said "Yes!" without a moment's reservation.

Joining Hadassah was really ideal for me; it was a way for me to meet people and, at the same time, do something helpful for what I hoped would become the Zionist State. "It's the answer to my prayers," I thought jubilantly.

I agreed to join and the woman on the other end of the telephone was delighted. Then she said: "Now let me see whether I have your name spelled correctly and your address," and she started to spell a name, but it was not *my* name at all; it wasn't even remotely similar. It was a completely different name.

Then it dawned on us both. The woman had gotten a wrong number when she called. She had called me by mistake!

After we laughed about the mix-up, she asked if I still wanted to join, and I said I certainly did, telling her that I was very happy the mistake had occurred. I gave her the necessary information, and she promised to call me when the next meeting was scheduled.

I attended and met lovely women my age who were very warm and welcoming. At this first meeting, which was held at Temple Emanuel in Newton Center, I sat beside a pretty, young, blonde woman named Gilda and I couldn't help but notice her. She was extremely friendly, and began to engage me in conversation. We began to talk, and we started a friendship that has lasted now for forty-seven years. She is my very best friend, and closer than a sister. There is a deep love that runs between us and will last as long as we live.

Beyond this extraordinary friendship, my membership in Hadassah brought me into the community. I hate to think what would have become of my life had the woman not dialed my number by mistake. But, who knows?

Maybe it wasn't a mistake at all.

—*Sybil Gladstone*

*Comment*

The more open we are to taking chances, the more apt we are to receive blessings.

*It* was Labor Day and Mother's Day all rolled into one when sisters Mary Luca, Catherine Naughton, and Toni Higgins at Methodist Hospital, Brooklyn amazingly gave birth to three beautiful babies just hours apart.

The multiple birth is believed to be the first time in the United States three sisters delivered on the same day.

And keeping the family theme: The obstreticians who delivered all three babies are brothers — Drs. Santo and Gary Fiasconaro.

The first of the three cousins was 7-pound, 4-ounce Daniel Vincent, born Friday morning by Caesarean section at New York Methodist to Mary Luce, 32, and her carpenter husband, Erik.

Mary's sister, Catherine Naughton, 31, gave birth later that morning to 6-pound, 2-ounce Kevin Patrick, also by C-section.

"The baby is tremendous. It's a terrific feeling to see a little baby born," said father Kevin. "And the fact that there are three of them at the same time, that's quite a coincidence."

The third sister, Toni Higgins, delivered 6-pound, 13-ounce girl Tyler, Friday night, completing the trifecta. She and her husband, Brian.

All three sisters say they conceived naturally nine months before.

"I don't quite know how it happened," Mrs. Naughton said. "I don't think anyone could have planned something like this."

The sisters had all been together May 4, 1996 for a niece's first Communion.

"We were all at Mary's daughter's Communion . . . and then three weeks later we were pregnant. So we must have eaten something . . . or drank something!" said Mrs. Higgins.

"For Mrs. Luca, this is her third child—and one that was unplanned.

"I was speechless. I was not expecting it in a million years."

So how is the family holding up?

"We're all tired, and the doctors look like they're a little beat," said Kevin Naughton. "And my mother-in-law really has her hands full, what with three daughters in the hospital and three babies heading home soon."

A computer search showed the previous record for same-day births by siblings was held by two sisters in Chicago in 1995.

—*Roger Field*

❧

### Comment

Sometimes the ordinary is exalted to the extraordinary only because of its placement in time.

*May* 30, 1983, was a glorious day and Sherry Vyverberg's spirits were high. She had just completed her exams, and her first year at Monroe Community College was finally over. Tall, with blue eyes and long blonde hair, Sherry had risen early and gotten out on the highway to pick up her boyfriend Keith Gandy, along with friends Greg Grant and Mike Jerocki. Together, they were looking forward to spending their Memorial Day weekend at Niagara Falls, an hour's drive from their hometown of Rochester, New York.

After stopping on the Canadian side of the falls for breakfast, the four young friends drove along the Niagara Parkway, winding along the bank of the Niagara River. Dazzled by the view, they parked their car beside the Toronto Power Station, an abandoned generating plant. Both Greg and Mike kept Keith company as he leaned against the old stone powerhouse. Recently he had broken his ankle; his leg was in a knee-high cast and he was on crutches.

Dressed in a new pink tracksuit, Sherry went alone to explore. She was drawn to the fine mist and the roar of the water, which cascaded over a wide crest to a boiling spume below. The churning water had a hypnotic effect on her and she wanted to get as close as she could.

A few feet from where she stood, a concrete observation platform beckoned. To get there, Sherry stepped around a metal railing and then walked across a short stretch of grassy bank onto the narrow observation ledge that hung twenty feet over the water. Standing just feet from the crest of the falls, Sherry stood mesmerized by the furious turbulence below that roared like muffled thunder and threw up a perpetual cloud of spray. Sherry marveled at the sense of exhilaration the falls gave her; she knew that she was peering over the rim of one of the seven wonders of the world. What she did not know was that below were some of the most dangerous rapids in the world, where 700,000 gallons of water fell every second from the 2,100-foot-wide crest.

Sherry's attention was drawn to the water that spilled from a sluiceway of the old powerhouse, just six meters below her. Carefully she leaned over to look at it. In that instant, she lost her balance and plunged headfirst into the forty-degree rapids.

"She's in the water!" screamed Mike, who had seen Sherry topple over the edge. Greg scrambled down the bank. "Where is she?" he shouted. "I can't find her!"

Sherry felt the shock of hitting the cold water, which pulled at her with enormous force. Somehow she was able to hold her breath under water and suddenly she was shot back to the surface. Keith spotted her just before she was sucked down again. "She's downstream!" he yelled. Gasping for air, Sherry made a frantic effort to reach the shore as the current pulled her into calmer waters. But she was thirty feet farther from shore and moving rapidly toward the crest of the falls.

Greg scaled the cliff and raced along the bank. When he caught up with Sherry, he dove into the frigid waters. He managed to swim out five meters before the torrential rapids overwhelmed him and forced him to make his way back to shore.

Meanwhile the water continued to slap at Sherry's face and shoulders. She felt the relentless pull of the river grow fiercer. In an attempt to stay afloat and to stop swallowing water, she quickly rolled over onto her back.

From a distance, the young men were shouting, "Hang on! We'll get you!" but Sherry couldn't hear their voices over the pounding waters. What she heard instead was her own loud voice praying to God. "I'm young," she pleaded, "please don't take me now!" Sherry remembered the beautifully wrapped gifts that she had placed in the deep recesses of her closet, each awaiting an appropriate occasion. Mugs for Dad and Gramps for Father's Day; a bank as a graduation gift for Wesley, her brother; and an Anniversary Waltz music box for her parents. "How sad those gifts would make them now," she thought.

Morbid thoughts rushed through Sherry's mind and paralyzed her body with fear. But in a monumental act of determination, Sherry realized she could not give in. Instead she drew on her inner reserves to calm down.

"I've just got to trust in God," she said, and then she continued to pray that her friends would somehow manage to save her.

Meanwhile Keith threw down his crutches and hobbled to the parkway. There he tried valiantly to flag down someone who might be able to help. The first vehicle just drove on by, but the second one stopped.

Pete Quinlan, Joe Camisa, and John Marsh were ironworkers who had been driving from their nearby work site. Their normal route had been changed to one-way, so they took a detour. They had forgotten their hard hats at the site and were on their way back to retrieve them when John noticed a man hopping up and down on one foot. Thinking there had been some accident, John rolled down his window and called out, "What's wrong?"

"There's a girl in the water! A girl in the water!" shouted Keith. John jumped out of his truck and ran down to the riverbank. At first, he saw only rushing water. Then he spotted Sherry's head, which looked like a beach ball some 300 feet out.

"She's way out!" yelled John. "We're never going to get out there." As a native of the area, he knew what Sherry was up against, and he even thought she might be done for. But as he witnessed her being swept downstream he thought, "I'd rather jump in than watch her go over the falls and spend the rest of my life second-guessing myself."

"I do a lot of fishing here," said John to his co-workers. John had grown up alongside Niagara Falls. Being an expert fisherman, he had rope in the back of the truck and he knew the patterns of the rapids. "Out where she is," he said, "the current is going to the falls. But if I cast out there, nine times out of ten my line drifts inside the weir, down by our powerhouse. If she doesn't go over the wall, she'll come drifting in to the powerhouse."

But he had to act quickly. Sherry was now only 245 meters from the brink of the falls. If she got carried through the intake gates to the turbines, she would be cut to ribbons. Once the current swept her over the weir, it would indeed be hopeless.

John Marsh and his co-worker Pete Quinlan were in the habit of working together. Immediately they went into gear as a team, grabbing rope from the back of the truck and knotting it together. John tied one end of the rope around his waist as Pete and Joe secured the other end to the steel railing of the bridge. John looked at the 175-foot drop below him, then yelled "Now!" and in a flash he jumped into the rapids.

The violent appetite of the current sucked John under, until he managed to thrust himself upward and stay afloat. The chill of the water slowed his movements, but he used all the energy and stamina he was able to muster and swam forward. Feeling the pull of the eighty-foot rope now fully extended, John called desperately to Sherry, who was now trying to reach him.

"Don't let me miss her," he begged. Sherry was still on her back, her long blonde hair floating behind her. John stretched every part of his body as he made a desperate lunge with his hand. Sherry was moving quickly as the current pulled her away from the weir. There was now just an inch between the two of them, one tied to a rope, the other boundless, floating rapidly downstream. "Don't let me miss her," John prayed again, then with one last attempt he stuck out his hand. This time, instead of coming up with only air, he caught the tips of Sherry's long hair and clutched it in his hand. "Thank God," gasped Sherry through her exhaustion. With her teeth chattering and her lips numb and blue, she looked at John, who had wrapped her in his arms and was pulling her in. She managed to say, "Thank you, too."

It was a feat getting both John and Sherry back to shore. Ambulances waited to treat Sherry for shock and hypothermia. She was released within two hours but in that time, the news media had gotten word of the miraculous rescue. Once John Marsh saw that Sherry was safe in the ambulance, he got into his vehicle with his buddies, ready to drive off. Canadian police officer Constable Caddis hailed him down and got his name. Now all those who wanted to bestow accolades had a name attached to the heroic deed. John Marsh did in fact receive tributes from Canadian and American politicians. He received a letter from President Ronald Reagan, who commended him for his heroism. Marsh went on to be awarded ten medals and plaques, including the Carnegie Medal, the ITT American Character Award, and the Royal Canadian Humane Association bronze medal, along with the Star of Courage from the governor general. "Why all the fuss?" John Marsh asks.

"So much of my rescue hinged on coincidence," Sherry is quoted as saying. "If John hadn't gone back for his crew's hard hats, if his normal route hadn't been changed to one-way, if he hadn't known the area so well or had a rope in his truck, I wouldn't be here today."

*Comment*

The distance between life and death is always one inch. We need the hand of God to bridge the gulf and pull us through.

*I*n 1947, I was riding the New York subway late one night, on my way home to Brooklyn from the evening session at Hunter College in Manhattan. I had gotten on the BMT line at Thirty-fourth Street, and noted with just a little chagrin that the subway was practically empty, with just a handful of people scattered throughout the car. I wasn't too concerned, though—this was the 1940s and subway incidents were uncommon. Still, I felt a little uncomfortable being one of the few passengers in the car.

One stop later, at Twenty-third Street, a gentleman got on the train, and I felt relieved that there would be another presence in the subway car. My relief, however, turned to uneasiness when he chose to sit in the seat immediately adjoining mine.

"Now why did he do that?" I wondered, distressed. "The entire subway car is practically empty, and yet he decides on a seat so close to mine. How strange!"

I peered into his face anxiously, and was reassured to see a mild-mannered man, with a pleasant countenance and an amiable manner. Rather than appear threatening, he seemed almost meek and timid.

"Ah! That's it! He's scared of the empty subway car himself! He's huddling close to *me* for comfort!"

I almost laughed.

In truth, he did not look like the average brash, aggressive American I often encountered on the subways.

"Maybe he's a foreigner," I mused.

My suspicions were confirmed seconds later when he withdrew a foreign-language newspaper and spread it out on his lap.

"That's it, then!" I reassured myself. "No need to worry, he's harmless." I settled back into my seat and returned to my book.

At the next stop—Fourteenth Street—a middle-aged woman boarded the train. Her head swiveled back and forth as she examined the nearly empty subway car. Then she, too, began to wend her way in the general direction of where I and the man were sitting.

She's going to sit nearby, too, I decided.

But to my surprise, she didn't even select an adjoining seat. Instead, she eased herself into the same seat as the foreign gentleman.

"Now that's peculiar," I thought. "The whole car is practically empty and she has to sit right next to a strange man, and real close at that."

I began to watch the woman with interest.

She peered over the man's shoulder to see what he was reading. And then she began to address him in a language in which I was not fluent, but which I could certainly identify.

She was speaking to him in Yiddish.

I didn't know Yiddish, but I did have an excellent command of German, which is quite similar. So I was able to follow the dialogue with very little difficulty.

"Where are you from . . . originally?" she inquired.

The man named a country in Eastern Europe.

"What city?" she asked.

He answered again, noncommittally, but beginning to look confused by the interrogation.

"What did you do . . . before the war?"

He named his profession.

"Look at me. Look *at* me!" she commanded. "Don't you recognize me anymore?"

They were husband and wife.

They had been separated in 1938 at the outset of World War II. Each had endured the horrors of different concentration camps and, at the war's end, each had assumed that the other was dead.

Each had made his way alone to New York City to begin a new life.

And they had found each other, nine years later, on a subway car on the BMT line.

As the reunion (which caused a sensation in New York and was reported widely in all the local newspapers) unfolded before my disbelieving, tear-filled eyes, I understood what force had compelled the woman to take the seat immediately adjoining the man's.

But what about *me?* I wondered, as my subway stop came around the bend and it was time, regretfully, for me to disembark.

Why had both chosen to sit next to *me?* What was my role supposed to be in this drama and what was my purpose?

As a very young woman, I didn't know. Today, some fifty years later, I think I do.

Perhaps I was placed there to serve as a witness. And perhaps I needed at a tender young age to learn a thing or two. To be imbued, from an early age on, with the sense of mystery and excitement and awe that such a tableau inspires.

And, having witnessed such an incredible "coincidence" unfold before my very eyes, to stand at the threshold of life knowing clearly that with God . . . all things are possible.

—*Ruth Fisher*

❧

### Comment
To be witness to a miracle is a miracle, too.

*om* Stone* first met the blonde at a mechanic's shop in Las Vegas where their respective cars were being fixed. He chatted her up with animation, hoping that she was as attracted to him as he was to her.

She wasn't.

When he asked her out, she brusquely said no.

Tom shrugged his shoulders in disappointment, but took the rejection well. At least he had tried, and it wasn't as if the two traveled in the same social circles. He would probably never see her again.

He was wrong.

One month later, Tom noticed a car parked on the shoulder of a road, its hood up, signifying trouble. He stopped to offer his help.

It was the blonde.

Once again, he felt the strong pull of attraction towards her. Once again, he asked her out. Once again, despite his obvious virtues (and mechanical aptitude, for he had indeed been able to locate the source of the car's trouble and rapidly repair it), she brusquely refused. Once again, Tom took her rejection well, and they parted ways.

But not for long.

One year later, on a different highway in a different part of town, Tom was riveted by the sight of a car on fire. He pulled up quickly behind the one that was ablaze, and discovered that it belonged to none other than . . . the blonde!

The scenarios of previous times were replicated faithfully. Tom successfully doused the fire, and then asked her out. Once again, the blonde said no.

Three years later on a bridge in San Francisco, Tom stopped to help victims of a multiple car accident. Surprise! One of them was . . . the blonde.

This time, even *she* was impressed by the coincidences that kept bringing them together, and — finally! — agreed to a date.

They arranged to meet at a restaurant in town, and Tom was elated.

His elation was short-lived.

The blonde never put in an appearance. After waiting for more than two hours at the appointed place and time, Tom concluded that she was a "no-show" and had rejected him again.

After that, Tom quit stopping at the scenes of car accidents. And he hasn't encountered the blonde since.

ↄ৽৵৵৽

### Comment

When I first read this story (which originally appeared in the *San Francisco Chronicle*), I was bitterly disappointed. I had had visions of the two sailing off into the sunset in sheer bliss. What was the point, after all, of this unusual series of coincidences, if not to bring the two together in matrimony? I was very annoyed at the unsatisfactory resolution of this tale. I never thought of transcribing the story, because it had no real conclusion, I thought, and therefore lacked inherent value. But the story kept nibbling away at my consciousness, and troubled me greatly. So I began to ask others what they thought of this tale. And one wise woman said, "Maybe the story isn't over yet." Hmm . . .

Another soul offered, "Maybe this story demonstrates what can happen if you are *not attuned* to coincidences. The blonde didn't heed their message. The script would have been different had she opened her heart to them. But we are, after all, given free will, and she made her choice."

*The* late afternoon sun was quickly descending on Linda Carlisle's hometown in central Ohio. It was December, and snow was falling lightly on the mile-and-a-half stretch to the high school. Mountainous snowbanks lined both sides of the road. Such a scene, where time almost seems to stand still, might have been painted by Grandma Moses. That was certainly the look of Linda's town thirty years ago.

Linda, with her flute tucked tightly under her arm, was late for band practice. To make matters worse, she had forgotten her mittens. She hustled as fast as the slippery terrain underfoot would permit her. And it was the time of year when it gets dark early.

Linda walked at a fast clip. Although she was tall for her seventeen years, she was beginning to run out of energy—the frigid air was sapping her strength. She could see her own breath coming out in short puffs. She had to slow down. Suddenly she saw that she had company. It came in the form of an enormous dog that bounded over the snowbank. The dog was so big its back came up to Linda's waist. He placed himself between Linda and the snowbanks. With the side of his husky body, the dog kept pushing Linda toward the street.

Linda was a little frightened. "Move away," she kept repeating to the dog in a firm voice. She didn't dare antagonize him because of his size. In the quiet street her words reverberated through the cold air. But the dog paid no attention to her stern commands. Refusing to obey, he continued to press his body against hers, pushing her away from the snowbanks and the rows of houses behind them.

Just as Linda quickened her pace to get away from the dog, a man with bright red hair and a demonic look in his eyes leaped from behind a snowbank. He lunged for Linda. The dog, who stood between the stranger and Linda, jumped on the man and pinned him to the ground. This action gave Linda the necessary seconds to escape.

The terrifying stranger was no match for the huge dog that was now gripping his leg in its jaws. Kicking himself free, the man scrambled over the snowbank and disappeared.

Linda was now ahead on the road, panting for breath. She still had a half mile to go when the dog reappeared, seemingly from nowhere. Once again, the dog pressed himself against Linda—this time on her left side so that he was protecting her from passing cars. She did not try to push the dog away this time. Overcome with gratitude, she patted the dog on its head. "Thank you," she said with heartfelt appreciation. And she meant it. "Thank you," she repeated.

Together they walked side by side until they reached the school. It was now so late that the door to the main entrance was locked. But she could hear the band practicing inside. Linda went around to the band door in the rear. She pounded loudly while the dog sat faithfully in the snow by her side. Eventually, one of the girls in the band opened the door.

"My goodness, Linda!" the girl exclaimed. "You look like you've just seen a ghost! Is there anything wrong?" It was difficult for Linda to speak. When she did, she described her harrowing encounter with the man on the road. "And this dog saved me," she said, as she turned to where the dog was sitting.

But the dog was no longer there. Nor was it anywhere in sight.

Linda knew, somehow, that she would never meet her four-legged savior again. For several months she kept perusing books about dogs in the school and town libraries. She wanted to know if there was a type of dog that protects people from harm. Or was it, as she suspected, one of a kind?

Linda is now forty-five and no longer lives in that small Ohio town. Despite all the research and the dozens of inquiries she has made over the years, she has never found a dog comparable to the one she encountered on that lonely cold night in the snow almost three decades ago.

❧

### Comment

One never knows the form in which a miracle will appear; therefore, we would do well to regard all that is around us with a degree of awe and wonder.

*R**abbi*** Shlomo Carlebach, one of the most original and inspired leaders in the Jewish community, was known throughout the world as "The Singing Rabbi." A great spiritual master in the mid-to-late twentieth century, he reached out to people of all persuasions. There were many beneficiaries of his fabled warmth and magnanimous heart. The stories told about him after his death in 1994 reflected a humanitarian who performed benevolent deeds of epic proportions.

Wherever he went—and he was a true globetrotter—he would always hug and kiss strangers and ask them for their names and phone numbers.

"Oh, holy brother!" (or holy sister, depending, of course, on the gender of his new friend), "it's awesome to meet you! I want to know all about you! Give me your name and phone number and I'll give you a call real soon."

Scraps of paper, slivers of napkins, ribbons of old menus, and tattered business cards were stuffed into his overflowing pants and coat pockets. Some people wondered, half cynically, if there was any point in giving their number to Rabbi Carlebach, or "Shlomo" as he was more affectionately known. "Probably throws the number out as soon as he gets home," some jaded souls would laugh.

It wasn't so. After his death, one family member estimated that at least *half a million names and numbers* had been accumulated—and saved—by Rabbi Carlebach during his lifetime.

Sometimes, his calls would come immediately on the heels of the initial meeting—just minutes or hours later. Sometimes they would come years later, long after the stranger had given up hope of ever hearing from the famous personality. But when they came, they always seemed to come at precisely the time when they were needed most.

In November 1997, at a weekend meeting of JACs (Jewish Alcoholics and Chemically Addicted), a man stood up and told this story about Shlomo Carlebach's famous phone calls:

"I had given him my phone number at a concert ten years before. He hadn't called, and I was sorely disappointed. But I was philosophical, not bitter. I figured he was a very famous, very busy guy, and how could he possibly call all those tens of thousands of strangers he met each year at the concerts and classes he gave throughout the world?

"I was wistful, but shy. I would have liked to have had the courage to call him up myself, but I didn't. My heart longed for a connection with this saintly man, but even though he seemed warm and unassuming, I was too timid to take the initiative myself.

"Ten years passed. I never saw him again. And then, one morning, the phone rang.

"I didn't want to answer it. I was in a very despondent state and didn't want to talk to *anyone*. But it rang repeatedly, insistently. The caller refused to give up. It must have rung twenty times. Reluctantly, I went to answer the phone.

"Hey, holy brother, what's happening?" the caller asked in a jovial, familiar voice.

It was Rabbi Shlomo Carlebach.

I was stunned. It had been ten years since he had first scribbled down my name.

"Shlomo," I asked, in total shock. "What made you call just now?"

"Well, I was looking for an old Bible which I haven't used for some time, and when I found it and opened it, a little piece of paper with your name and number fell out. I figured it was a sign from God I should give you a call!"

An electric jolt coursed through my body and into my very soul. "Shlomo," I said, staring at the noose that was dangling from the ceiling and at the chair underneath it which I had just prepared.

"You called just in time."

❦

## Comment

Even in the darkest moments of our soul there may very well be someone, somewhere holding the torch that can guide us back to life.

*O*n the last day of school, Liz, Jennifer, and Stephanie went out to dinner to celebrate. They ordered drinks, but there was no atmosphere of merriment. Like many public schoolteachers in inner-city Tampa, they were feeling the sobering effects of burn-out after yet another tough year.

Though normally a very sentimental bunch, they talked about how demoralized they felt at the end of this particular school session. "I haven't made a difference to anyone this year," said Stephanie.

"Oh, I'm sure you have," said Liz.

"Of course you have," said Jennifer.

Yet nobody seemed convinced. The three teachers paid their checks and with weak smiles they wished each other a good summer.

Stephanie Osborne headed home, feeling dejected and down. She feared bitterness; she feared that the daily realities of her job in the school system would eventually whittle away the idealism that fed her soul. As she drove she tried to boost her spirits with positive thoughts. "I am a seventh-grade language arts teacher in the inner city," she said to herself. "My strength is that I can relate to the students no one else gets along with. Just look at the work I've done with the 'at-risk' kids in the after-school mentoring program."

It was true—she *had* made a difference, at least in the life of Steve, the first student she had mentored. At first disruptive and belligerent, with her help he became thoughtful and caring. He had only been acting out because of a rough time at home. Stephanie knew that every child had a positive core that needed only to be revealed and allowed to grow. How good it had made her feel when Steve's grades improved and things began looking up for him.

But that had been two years ago. This time, nobody had hugged her to say good-bye on the last day of school, as Steve had. Somehow, the past two years had brought not only successes, but some failures as well— kids who slipped through the cracks.

Was she losing her touch? Was it really worth it after all? Was it just youthful idealism to believe that every being on earth has something unique and positive to offer?

She was ashamed by her thoughts, and as she drove she asked for a sign from above. And then, as she pulled into her driveway, she heard the telephone ringing. Who could it be at this hour? Quickly she parked and fumbled for her house keys as she tried to catch the phone before it was too late. She opened the door, ran inside, and picked up the receiver.

"Hello," she said, out of breath.

"Mrs. Osborne?" came a familiar though tentative voice on the other end. "It's Steve!"

Stephanie could not believe her ears. Her heart swelled as her former student went on to tell her that he was out of trouble, doing well in school, and employed. He said he had been thinking about her.

Steve could not have known how much that phone call meant to her. Stephanie went to bed that night with her spirits lifted, wondering if, just maybe, the next few years might bring a similar call from someone else.

❧

### Comment

A gift of gratitude often rekindles inspiration gone dim.

*T*he blue-green sea spread out before me like a blanket as I waded into the warm water of Lydgate Lagoon on the Hawaiian island of Kauai. Could a month in paradise help me heal?

I wasn't sure anything could.

Only a month before, I'd been lying in the hospital back home in New England, admitted for heart problems and exhausted from multiple sclerosis. "My daughter and I are supposed to be on a plane to Kauai at this very moment!" I had told the doctor.

"Don't worry," my twenty-three-year-old daughter Dorene had reassured me. "We'll just postpone the trip. It's not the end of the world."

But it felt like it.

At forty-nine, with my divorce behind me, I wanted to believe I still had a lot of living to do. But instead, my heart was racing, my left side was weak—and I felt that I was falling apart.

Seventeen long days had passed in the hospital as I lay in bed wondering if I'd ever feel strong again. But this trip would do more for me than I could ever have imagined.

The sun was on my face as I fed the tropical fish that swam below the surface. I wanted to dive into the glassy blue, but my doctor's words echoed in my mind. "Take it easy," he had warned.

I'm not much of a swimmer anyway. Once, as a young girl, I went swimming in a lake and got a cramp in my leg. Before I knew it, I was under. I panicked, feeling that my lungs were ready to burst. Finally, someone pulled me out. But ever since that time, I couldn't put my head underwater. I'd just paddle and float.

So I paddled and floated out, and when I could no longer feel the sandy floor, I just let the water support my body.

I watched a man swim to shore to look after his three children while his wife went in, scuba gear in hand. Then I kept floating out—about 100 feet—to the deepest part of the lagoon.

There may have been ten other swimmers, or rather, snorkelers, their breathing straws skimming and bobbing in the water. But my vision was drawn farther out to a figure whose jerking movements had suddenly caught my eye.

"Hey," I thought. "That's the mother of those children!"

Without making a sound, the woman threw up her arm, which twisted like a corkscrew. And she was gasping as she tried to yank off her diving mask.

Instantly, I knew I was witnessing an epileptic seizure. I had seen one years ago. And now, there was only still water where the young mom had been.

My mind went blank as my body took over. I paddled over as fast as I could, my heart pounding. And then, without thinking, I dove beneath the water.

I don't even remember pulling the woman to the surface. But suddenly, there I was, floating, holding onto her with my stronger right arm to keep her afloat. And then I found my voice and screamed, "Help!"

None of the snorkelers heard me. So I kept screaming, trying to keep the woman—convulsing and clutching me—from pulling us both under.

On the shore, I saw Dorene jump at the sound of my voice, and she started shouting, too. And then the woman's husband suddenly realized what was happening.

"Ellen," he cried. "Ellen!" The sound of his plaintive cries made my heart break.

"I can't wait for help," I thought. "We have to get to shore." So with my weak left arm, I swam with all my might. Will we make it? I panicked. But then I saw a man swimming quickly toward us.

Panting, he reached us. "She's having a seizure!" I cried.

"Take her legs," he shouted, and together we towed her to shore.

When my feet finally touched bottom, I called to the crowd: "Get a doctor!" As it turned out, there was one on the beach, who performed CPR and emptied her lungs of water. Within minutes, she and her family had disappeared in an ambulance.

Standing in the water, I realized for the first time what had happened, and I started to sob. My fellow rescuer came toward me. "You saved her life," he said.

"*We* did," I replied.

"You know," he said, "strangest thing. . . . I'd postponed this vacation because I was ill. I was just wading in the water when . . ."

Then I told him my own story.

For a moment, we just stared at each other, knowing we had shared something incredible.

Maybe it wasn't just a coincidence that we were both there to save that woman, I thought. Maybe, just maybe, God wanted to give us something: the feeling of strength when we felt weak. To show us something: that we could do something wonderful for another person even when we weren't sure what we could do for ourselves.

We called the hospital and learned that Ellen had been released. She never knew that the stranger who reached out to her that day was me.

I think about Ellen a lot. Whenever I feel tired or weak, I remember the feeling of my legs and arms moving furiously and the sensation of power taking hold.

If I could pull a woman out of the ocean, I can do anything!

If you asked Ellen, she'd probably tell you that I was her guardian angel.

But if you ask me, I'd have to say *she* was *mine*.

—*Arlene Nunes*

### Comment

When we reach beyond ourselves to care for another, we are often led past our own fears and limitations.

"*W*ho the heck keeps on doing this?" Wayne Morgan* bellowed at his wife as he stomped into the kitchen early one fall morning, laden with groceries, shaking the rain from his overcoat.

"What're you talking about, honey?" his wife Linda asked absently, concentrating on the pancakes she was skillfully flipping.

"Some idiot keeps tampering with the garbage cans. For the last few days, somebody keeps moving one of the garbage cans from the front yard into the alleyway right under the bedroom windows. Is this some crazy kind of joke? I keep moving the garbage can back into the front yard, and the next day it's in the alley again!"

"Listen, honey," his wife soothed, "I know it must be annoying to have to keep on moving the garbage can back to the front, but really it's no big deal."

"Yeah," he grumbled, "it's no big deal, you're right, but still I find it extremely aggravating! And it just seems so senseless, so stupid!"

"Well, did the same thing happen again just now? What's the fate of the wandering garbage can today?" Linda teased.

"Yeah, well that's what got me going. Last night, I moved the garbage can into the front yard, and this morning when I left for the supermarket it was back in the alley. So I returned the can to the front, and

161

when I got home from shopping, there it was in the alley again!"

"Well, at least you're finally getting some exercise!" his wife tried to joke.

"Well, I didn't move it back this time because I was carrying the groceries," Wayne said. "I'll go do it in a minute after I have my coffee."

"Listen, when you get a chance," Linda asked, casually changing the subject, "can you please fix the guardrail on the baby's window? It's very loose and now that she's crawling around and standing, I'm afraid she can hoist herself up to the window seat and who knows what could happen?"

"Oh my god," Tom shrieked. "You didn't tell me the guardrail was broken! I opened the window this morning and I took the baby out of the crib before I left for the market."

The two exchanged a frantic look and raced to the bedroom.

The guardrail was gone from the window, the baby missing from the room.

Linda screamed and slumped into a chair. His heart palpitating with fear, Tom willed himself to look out the open window, expecting the worst.

A choking sob escaped from his lips — half-gasp, half-benediction, as his eyes widened in amazement at the scene below.

Two stories beneath the open bedroom window, a familiar cooing sound came from the baby, whose little arms were flailing energetically as she tried to extricate herself from the cushion that had buffered her fall.

She was nestled in the garbage can filled with the soft leaves that her father had raked and collected the week before.

❧

### Comment
Sometimes the cure arrives before the curse, but blinded as we mere mortals often tend to be, we fail to recognize either one for what they truly are.

*I*n the winter of 1977, Miriam Altschul* moved with her husband and baby to Brooklyn from the Bronx neighborhood where she had grown up as a child.

The move was not an easy one. Every street, every signpost, every store in the old Bronx neighborhood had been familiar and known to Miriam. Most were replete with special memories and nostalgic moments. She knew all the local people and considered many of them to be her close friends.

In Brooklyn, she didn't know a soul.

Still, as her practical husband had convincingly persuaded her, the old Bronx neighborhood was deteriorating, and it was no longer an ideal place to raise a child. Flatbush, on the other hand, was a flourishing section bursting at the seams with young families like theirs, pulsating with energy and vitality. It boasted fine schools and excellent shopping and would provide them with the quality of life they sought.

But without friends, life felt hollow indeed.

As winter wore on, Miriam grew melancholy and despondent. "Perhaps it was a mistake to move to an apartment building where the living is so anonymous," she thought. "Everyone is holed up in their own individual cave. Maybe a private house would have been a better idea," she conjectured.

"And a move smack dead in the middle of winter! What were we thinking?" she berated herself.

The frigid temperatures, icy conditions, and perpetual snowfalls of what was a particularly hard winter that year kept her prisoner indoors with the baby much of the time. "At least if we had moved during the fall or waited for springtime, I could have gone out to the park and met other young mothers there," she thought with rue.

Miriam was a warm, sociable, gregarious type who liked and required company. Without it, she withered. She felt increasingly depressed, imprisoned in a cocoon of intense isolation. "I need a friend," she thought in desperation.

One morning, when the temperatures had climbed a bit and the sun shone brightly, Miriam decided to venture outdoors with her child. Impulsively, she did something that was not characteristic of her. She lived on the second floor of the apartment building and, young and nimble, she normally took the stairs down to the lobby. It was faster than waiting for the elevator, which was slow and ominously creaky. But on this particular morning, some inner voice told her to choose the elevator instead, and she waited patiently for it to arrive. When she opened the door, she saw a young woman with rosy cheeks and flashing eyes, cuddling a child her son's age.

She had found her friend.

The vivacious young woman smiled at Miriam invitingly and introduced herself, bubbling: "You must be the new tenant! I heard you moved in, and I wanted to drop by and say hello, but I'm so sorry, I just didn't get the chance. Hi, my name's Toby Green*. What's yours? Where are you from? How do you like it here so far? Do you have friends or relatives living here? No? Oh, my, that's terrible! Are you stuck inside all winter just like me? Well, the kids look like they're around the same age—let's get together then!"

Toby not only befriended Miriam, she took her under her wing. She shepherded her around the neighborhood, acquainting her with its different shopping districts and other facilities, introducing her to various people, escorting her to meetings of women's volunteer groups, and in general making sure that Miriam's presence was known to the community at large. The two became inseparable and went everywhere together—doing errands, going on outings with the boys, exercising, eating out, and more.

Toby proved to be a veritable blessing in Miriam's life, banishing the loneliness that had hung over her like a dark cloud. Miriam was soon able to successfully integrate herself into the new neighborhood and create the social life she longed to have. "I owe so much to Toby," Miriam often thought with gratitude. "She's helped me a lot. What would I have done without her?"

One year later, Toby moved to Toronto, Canada, and Miriam never saw her again.

In 1994, Pinchos Altschul, Miriam's seventeen-year-old son, graduated from high school and decided to pursue additional studies at a prestigious institution in Israel. It would be the first time in his life that he was away from his family for any significant period, and the first time he would be on his own in a country frequently besieged by bomb scares and terrorist attacks.

It was also the first time in his life that he would be heading for a new school without any friends in tow. And for a young boy of seventeen, it was that scenario that produced the greatest anxiety of all.

Pinchos, a friendly, outgoing boy, had always had a large circle of friends and an active social life. But although several of his high school classmates in New York had chosen to study in Israel, they had struck out in separate directions, and each had selected a different institution. None had opted for his school. Although no one in his family was worried about Pinchos, knowing his capacity to make friends easily, he himself was filled with misgivings. A foreign country . . . a new school . . . no family . . . all alone. "I hope I find a good friend soon," he thought wistfully.

The boy had rosy cheeks and sparkling eyes, a warm smile, and a sunny personality. Pinchos bumped into him one morning in the corridor of the dormitory, and the boy flashed him an impish grin. "Hey, are you the new kid down the hall?" he bubbled. "I heard about you and wanted to come say hi but I just didn't get around to it. My name is Sholom. I'm also new here and I bet you're feeling a little down and lonely and of course that's natural but I'm also new here so how about we combine forces and do stuff together OK?"

Sholom took Pinchos under his wing, introduced him to the other guys in the dorm, taught him the ropes, shepherded him around Jerusalem, and in many different ways helped him adapt to the new and different rhythms of dormitory life. Because of his friendship with Sholom, Pinchos adjusted easily, thrived in school, and had a valuable growth experience that would heavily influence the course of his future academic career. Most important of all, he was happy.

"I owe so much to Sholom," Pinchos often thought. "How can I ever repay him for all that he's given me? Maybe, when school's over, I can invite him to New York for the summer . . ."


"Hey, Mom," Sholom asked his mother a few days after his return home to Toronto in June. "Would it be OK if I vacationed in New York this summer?"

"What would you do there? Where would you stay?" his mother asked.

"I was invited by this kid from school. We were very close friends in Israel."

"Really? What's his name?" his mother asked.

"Pinchos Altschul."

"Altschul . . . that's an unusual name . . . could he possibly be related to Miriam Altschul?"

"That's his mother's name. Do you happen to know her?"

Silently, his mother walked to the closet where she stored old photographs and withdrew an ancient-looking album whose pages were yellowing. She motioned Sholom to her side and pointed to a faded photograph of two young women in outdated shirtdresses, arms linked around each other warmly, with a pair of cherubic toddlers sitting side by side on their laps.

Sholom recognized the spirited-looking woman with the flashing eyes; it was his mother, of course. And the child enfolded in her embrace was him.

But who was the other pretty woman she was hugging so affectionately, and what was the name of the little boy on *her* lap?

"Pinchos Altschul," Toby Green of Toronto said softly, wiping away a tear. "His mother, Miriam, was my best friend in New York in 1977. Without knowing it, Sholom, it seems as if you and your childhood playmate have reenacted a script that was written almost two decades ago."

#### Comment

Whether they be blood feuds or love stories, certain forces that are set into motion in one generation are often repeated in the next, and seeds sown in the distant past bear fruit in a future we can never envision.

*T*hroughout her childhood, Sara Ain Flascher had sustained her fair share of bumps, bruises, scrapes, and cuts, but she had never endured the painful sting of a bee. Thus, she was completely unaware of the fact, and had never had cause to suspect, that she was allergic — extremely allergic — to bee venom.

When she was subjected to her very first bee sting, she was already an adult, oblivious to the danger that awaited her and completely unprepared for it.

She felt the sudden stab early one fall afternoon, as she chatted animatedly with friends whom she was visiting at their home in Newburgh, New York.

"Ouch!" she yelped in distress as the stinger penetrated her skin. Her finger immediately began to throb, and she felt it grow tender.

"Kurt!" she called out to her husband. "Come quick! I think I've been stung by a bee."

Kurt ran to her side to reassure her and downplay the effects of bee stings. He, too, was unaware of the grave peril his wife faced, a peril that would grow more serious by the minute.

"Don't worry; it's nothing," he soothed. "I know people who've had dozens of bee stings and it's really nothing to get upset about. The pain will subside soon."

But the pain increased rather than diminished, and the finger began to swell to ominous proportions. Then Sara's arm began to throb.

"Kurt," Sara asked in alarm, "you know I get weekly allergy shots for all the things I'm allergic to; could I possibly be allergic to bee venom as well?"

No physician had ever warned Sara of the possibility, so neither of them realized that this was indeed what they were dealing with—a serious allergic reaction to a bee bite.

Just then, the doorbell rang. The friend they were visiting, who had been anxiously hovering over Sara, reluctantly turned to answer the door. "Be right back," she promised.

A middle-aged woman was standing on the threshold with a worried look on her face.

"I'm so sorry to disturb you," she apologized in a soft voice, "but I live down the block and my mother has Alzheimer's disease and she wandered away from home and we're looking for her everywhere and wondering if perhaps one of the neighbors has seen her or taken her in and I feel so guilty because I should have been watching her more carefully but I was distracted by an emergency phone call from a patient of mine and . . ."

Sara's friend interrupted the woman in mid-sentence. *"Patient?"* she exclaimed with excitement. "Are you a doctor, by any chance?"

The woman nodded a puzzled yes.

Sara's friend pulled her into the house. "Please take a look at my guest. She was just bitten by a bee and seems to be having an unusual reaction . . ."

The doctor rushed in.

Sara's arm was now swollen and the finger had ballooned.

The doctor rapidly pulled out the stinger, then rushed around the kitchen using household supplies like baking soda and ice to pack Sara's hand. Then she took a second look at her and hustled her into a car, speeding to her office—a minute away—where she administered an injection, which, she explained, was an antidote to the bee venom.

Later, after the excitement had died down, the swelling had begun to recede, and the Flaschers had expressed their thanks and appreciation effusively, the doctor said thoughtfully, "You know, Mr. Flascher, the rapid intervention I was able to administer saved your wife from serious consequences. If I hadn't rung the doorbell when I did, who knows what might have happened?"

Many years after the incident, the Flaschers still retell the story with awe and gratitude. It's a "small miracle," they say, one they'll surely remember for the rest of their lives.

~~~

### Comment
Those seeking help from you may very well come to be the source of your salvation.

$\mathcal{C}$*olleen* looked at the date on her calendar and sighed. A lifetime before—eighteen years, to be exact—she had given birth to a baby girl and given her up for adoption.

Throughout the years, the thought of this child had haunted her: was she smart, was she pretty, was she healthy, was she happy? Now, it was getting close to the child's eighteenth birthday. By law in Canada she was finally free to conduct a search to discover her daughter's destiny. Did she dare?

She decided to make a move, albeit a small one. Though she had since moved to a town hundreds of miles away, Colleen called the newspaper in the town of Alberta, Canada, the baby's birthplace.

"Let me speak to your classified section," she asked the operator at the Alberta *Times*. "I'd like to place an ad."

"Sure," said the operator, "what's your message?"

It was such a long shot, Colleen considered hanging up. But timing was critical; the ad needed to appear on the exact date of her daughter's birth.

"Happy birthday," she began. Then she provided the name she had given her daughter when she gave her up for adoption eighteen years before, along with a simple message announcing her search and her phone number in the remote town where she lived.

That might have been the end of the story, if it hadn't been for an editor toiling late in the newsroom who noticed Colleen's ad. "There's something going on here," he said to himself.

That very same day, a woman named Jodi Mitchell had called the Alberta *Times*. Although she did not live in Alberta, the woman was hoping to find somebody who might. Eighteen years ago, Jodi had been adopted. The only information she had about her adoption proceeding was that she was born in Alberta. With the hope that her biological mother still lived in Alberta, the young woman had placed an ad announcing her search.

Immediately, the editor picked up the phone and called Colleen. It was almost 11 P.M. Colleen became concerned when she learned who it was. "Is there a problem?" she asked.

"No!" replied the editor, "it's just that there's a coincidence here that's too big to ignore. There's another ad in here that sounds, you know . . . similar to yours." Colleen got goose bumps when he told her about the other ad. With a shaking hand, she wrote the number down and called the young woman.

Indeed, Jodi Mitchell turned out to be Colleen's daughter. Who would have guessed they would place identical ads, in the same distant paper, on the same day? Like mother, like daughter.

### Comment

Know that there is a master weaver bringing together those who are meant to be with one another.

*W*ayne grabbed his swimsuit and loped towards the door. "Bye, Mom, I'm going to my friend's house," he said.

"Hold on just one minute!" Pat said, jumping in front of her teenage son. She looked for his eyes under his baseball cap. "Now, when will you be coming home?"

Wayne rolled his eyes. This was a familiar routine. He told her he would be back the following night and kissed her on the cheek.

But Mom wasn't so easily put off. With a shake of her finger and a smile, Pat said, "I want you to call me by noon tomorrow." She handed him a scrap of paper so he could write down the friend's number. When he was gone, she placed the number on her headboard with the intention of taking it to work in the morning. How well she knew her Wayne.

The following day at work, Pat anticipated a call from her son. But noon turned into 1:00, which rolled into 2:00, and still he hadn't called. Pat shook her head knowingly. She worried in spite of herself. She fished through her wallet to retrieve the friend's number and then slapped her knee as she realized she had left it at home. "Now what do I do?" Pat fretted.

She was in a fix. She couldn't leave the office, but the thought of waiting to hear from her son on his teenage time clock was unsettling. She would be preoccupied with thoughts of Wayne and his well-being all day. Closing her eyes and willing herself to be calm, Pat tried to recall the numbers scribbled on the white piece of paper. As a shot in the dark she phoned the number she was best able to recall.

After two rings, a man answered.

"Hello," Pat said, timidly. "Is Wayne Brown there, by any chance?"

"Let's see, Wayne Brown, Wayne Brown . . ." the man repeated slowly, as if he was thinking. Pat debated hanging up.

"I don't seem to recall any Wayne Brown having come by today," he said.

Pat thanked the man quickly, explained that she had the wrong number, and was about to hang up when the man said, "How old is Wayne?" Pat looked at the phone quizzically. What a strange question! "How old?" she said. "Sixteen." She wished she hadn't answered, but something impelled her. Nevertheless, the man said he could not help her, and hung up. Pat decided dialing any more numbers was a bad idea, and tried to keep her mind on work.

Four hours later, a coworker answered the telephone and handed it to Pat. "Hello?" Pat said as she placed the receiver to her ear. Much to her relief, it was Wayne. His voice sounded incredulous. "Mom!" he cried, "how did you know to call me at the dentist's office?"

Pat stood up from her seat. "What are you talking about?" she laughed. With characteristic animation,

Wayne explained the story. "My friend needed to have his braces removed, and asked me to go along with him. I said, 'Why not?'

"I walk into the dentist's office," Wayne continued, "and my friend introduces me to this dentist I've never seen before. 'This is Wayne Brown,' my friend says, and the dentist says, 'Your mother is waiting for your call.'

"I thought the dentist was joking — I mean, how could he possibly know that? Then he tells me you had called his office. Now Mom, I didn't even know I'd be coming here, *so how in the world did you know?*"

It turns out that Pat had indeed dialed a "wrong number." The dentist was on a lunch break; he was in his little house behind the office. Ordinarily he would not be answering a phone, but this number rang on his private line so he picked it up.

This took place in Anchorage, Alaska, where there is a population of a quarter of a million people with an untold number of telephone lines crossing through. For Pat, though, she needed just one call, from her son, and by God, she got it.

❧

*Comment*

Although the umbilical cord is severed within the first few moments of life, its spiritual counterpart continues to pulsate forever, transmitting a stream of unspoken messages between mother and child.

*H*e was the runt of the litter — small, puny and sickly-looking, almost too feeble to stand on his weak legs, cowering in a dark corner of the barn.

"You don't want him," said Bill, the puppies' owner, brusquely, motioning toward the four robust ones tumbling in the hay. "Any one of those would be a better choice."

But my gaze remained fastened on the pitiful looking pup, who returned my glance with entreating eyes, and a soft, sweet expression that could melt the coldest of hearts.

"Does he have a name?" I asked.

"Listen, Johnny," Bill sighed, "I'm a good friend of your father's and I don't want to steer you wrong. I'm not even sure that pup is gonna make it."

*Like me,* I thought. They weren't sure that I was going to make it, either.

The previous year, at the age of thirteen, I had been diagnosed with leukemia, and I was now in remission. But I had been as fragile as the eight-week-old pup that now bounded over to me from across the room, licking my hand enthusiastically.

"Well, I'll be doggoned." Bill scratched his head. "He never did that before. He's such a shy, scared pup, 'fraid of everything and everybody. 'Fraid of his own shadow. Seems like he really likes you, though."

"We have something in common," I said wryly, more to myself than to Bill.

As I bent down and stroked the pup, I felt the strong connection surge through me.

"Does he have a name?" I asked again.

"Miracle," said Bill grimly. "Cause it sure is one that he's still alive; he was so sick the first few weeks."

"I'll take him."

Bill touched my shoulder in a gesture of compassion. "I don't want to see you getting hurt, Johnny. What if the pup dies on you? You've gone through a lot this year. I don't want you to suffer the pain of losing him. Take my advice; choose another pup, please!"

But I left the barn with Miracle cuddled in my arms. I wasn't called stubborn for nothing.

Over the years, Miracle proved that first appearances can be deceiving. He learned to be as feisty as me. His spirit turned into an indomitable one, and we taught each other how to fight: death, disease, other peoples' bad insights and poor judgments. There were precarious times in both of our lives, but we endured them together and triumphed over adversity. We survived.

Was ever a boy and his dog so connected like Miracle and me? He walked me to school along the rural roads of Maine where I lived, and then raced himself home; he was promptly outside the school building at 3 P.M. to escort me back. He slept at the foot of my bed, and his sleeping patterns matched mine exactly. He was keenly sensitive of my moods, inundating me with wet sloppy kisses when I was especially blue, fiercely protective when my siblings teased or taunted me.

"We are bonded forever, and we will be together always," I often fancifully thought.

"Forever" came to a crashing halt four years later. I had been accepted to a prestigious university in Boston and had received a scholarship I had tenaciously pursued and sorely needed. My dream had finally been achieved: I had been admitted into one of the most elite academic institutions in the world.

"What am I going to do about Miracle?" I wondered aloud to my mother one day, when I learned that students were required to live in the school's dormitory, where no pets were permitted.

"You have no choice," my mother said. "You'll have to leave him behind. I know it's hard for you to be parted from him, but you'll see him on Christmas vacation and at Easter."

My heart was heavy with grief as I said my final farewell to Miracle the day I left home. "I wish I could explain to you why I'm leaving," I told him sadly. "And I wish I could find a way to let you know I'm coming back. When I call, I'll have Mom put your ear to the receiver so you can hear my voice."

But I never got the chance, because the day after I left, Miracle was gone.

My mother broke the news to me gently, with a tremor in her voice.

Miracle had disappeared. He had gone out in the morning to roam the neighborhood in pursuit of canine adventures, but he had not faithfully returned in the evening, as he always had before.

An accident? I asked, throat tightening, body stiff with fear.

All the animal hospitals, shelters, and veterinarians in town had been called. Ditto for police stations, fire departments, and emergency medical services.

No one had seen Miracle.

A dognapping? I proposed.

My mother was dubious. It was true that Miracle was a beagle—a pure breed—but he was male and five years old. And besides, our sleepy little town was not exactly the kind of place where dognappers skulked and snatched prey.

So what could have happened to Miracle?

Everyone was mystified, my mother said.

But I . . . I was heartbroken.

"Hey, pal," I whispered, "we were a team, remember? Forever is supposed to be a long time."

I called my parents daily for several weeks to hear if Miracle had been found. But the news was never good, and "Not yet, Johnny" soon turned into "I don't think that he's alive, son."

I stopped calling.

When I came home for Christmas, Easter, and the summer holidays, I went looking for Miracle. All the favorite retreats we had haunted together — a favored fishing hole, a choice site in the woods, a verdant pasture where Miracle always romped joyously — all held no signs of him and yielded no clues. I walked the streets of my little town, anxiously asking everyone I encountered: "Have you seen my dog Miracle?"

But no one had seen him. "Not for months," they said.

"I think it's time that we accept that Miracle's really gone," my mother said.

"I can't accept that," I said. "Because it's not the truth."

One year later, I was in my dorm room at the university thinking about Miracle, when my roommate turned to me with a puzzled look.

"What's that noise?" he demanded, scowling.

"What noise?" I asked absently, engrossed in my thoughts and not hearing anything irregular.

"Like . . . a peculiar scratching sound. . . . Listen, don't you hear it, now?"

I raced to the door and flung it open wide.

He rushed into my arms with little whimpering cries, and I hugged him tight. There was no flesh on his skeletal frame, and his fur was matted with grime. His eyes looked dull and feverish, and his stance was unsteady. Despite the changes that a year on the road had wrought in his appearance, it was undeniably my beloved dog.

"This is your dog that disappeared a year ago in *Maine?*" demanded my roommate with incredulity. "How could that be? How could the dog travel so many hundreds of miles in all kinds of weather and survive? . . . But more important . . . how did he find his way to you in *Boston?* How is that possible?"

"Anything is possible," I whispered.

*"My God,"* my roommate shouted, "it's a miracle."

"No," I corrected gently, "it *is* Miracle!"

*C*harlene Wheatley was a cosmetics salesgirl at Bloomingdale's. For nine years she had worked at the Prescriptives counter, seeing thousands of faces and handling all sorts of customers from countries across the globe.

One day a tourist appeared at her counter. Since Charlene's sister-in-law is Japanese, she immediately detected the woman's Japanese accent, and understood how to put the woman at ease by speaking slowly and politely.

"May I help you?" she said with a smile, a bow, and a soft tone.

"I . . . would . . . like . . . skin . . . care," said the timid woman in halting English.

With patience and care, Charlene showed the woman the full line of Prescriptives products, explaining the benefits of each. Although it was not easy, the two women managed to communicate through nods, gestures, smiles, and a few words.

Charlene's courtesy obviously made a big impression on the woman, for she bought several products and then thanked Charlene repeatedly. "Thank you . . . thank you . . . for this time you spent with me," said the woman. She paid, bowed once more in gratitude, and left the counter.

Charlene was still smiling about the encounter when the woman appeared again, half an hour later. She had decided to stock up on all her items before returning to

Japan. "Happy to oblige," smiled Charlene. As she went about collecting the items, Charlene felt friendly enough with the woman to mention her Japanese sister-in-law. It was rare that Charlene actually shared anything of her personal life with her customers; her conversations almost always focused on the products.

"Oh yes?" responded the woman with surprise, looking up from her selections. "Oh yes!" Charlene said, giggling, emboldened by the woman's response. "I even know a few words of Japanese—like *Musashi*—that means samurai warrior." The woman giggled back. It was funny to hear such a familiar word spoken by an American.

"As a matter of fact," continued Charlene, "that's the name of my nephew." But Charlene had forgotten herself—she had forgotten to speak slowly. The woman looked confused. "Nephew," Charlene repeated. Then she had an idea—she pulled a picture of her beaming eight-year-old nephew out of her bag.

"See? Musashi, my nephew," said Charlene, and she handed the picture to the woman, expecting her to smile. But when the woman's eyes settled on the picture of the boy, her expression froze in shock. Her hand flew to her mouth and she shrieked.

"What is it?" cried Charlene.

Customers and salespeople alike all turned around at the sound of the loud voices as the woman continued to exclaim—"Can not be! Can not be! . . ."

Small Miracles II  ❧  185

"But you must tell me! What is it?" insisted Charlene. The woman finally seemed to catch her breath, and then spoke. "This boy," she said, pointing to the picture in her hand, *"he my godson!"*

In the best words she could muster, she tried to explain to Charlene that the boy's mother, Charlene's sister-in-law, had been her best friend back in Japan. The family had moved years ago and the two had lost contact over the years. In fact, she was now in New York trying desperately to find them.

"Thank you!" she said with a more radiant smile than any lipstick could ever give her. "Thank you!"

Within a matter of hours, best friends, godmother, and godchild were reunited.

ꙮ

*Comment*

From one nation to another runs a line that connects one heart to another.

*T*ommy Hoyt* heard the screams before he actually saw the scuffle. Then he realized that the flurry of movement his brain had barely registered a second ago wasn't an animated discussion, as he had assumed, but a furious struggle. On the other side of the subway car, a man was ripping a gold pendant from the neck of a young woman with an angelic face and startled sapphire eyes.

Everyone in the car seemed to freeze. Later, Tommy would reflect that what some people mistakenly attribute to apathy is actually a form of collective shell shock. Everyone seemed chilled, hardened into a kind of slow-motion freeze-frame. It wasn't that the passengers didn't care, it was that they simply couldn't move.

Tommy was the first to regain his wits. He shook himself out of his paralysis and moved toward the girl. She was still locked in battle with the mugger, feistily (or foolishly) refusing to surrender her necklace. "If only I can reach her before the guy gets it," he thought, pushing through the hordes of subway riders blocking his passage. But only a few feet away, he watched helplessly as the mugger gave a savage yank and succeeded in tearing the pendant off her neck. The train had just reached the station and the mugger ran out the open door onto the subway platform.

"Help!" the victim cried feebly.

Tommy dashed out the door in pursuit of the thief. He caught up with him at the end of the platform and tackled him. He grabbed the pendant out of his hand, as the mugger slipped out of his grasp. "At least I got the necklace back," Tommy thought with satisfaction, "even if the mugger did get away."

Tommy wondered what the angelic blonde would say when he made his victorious return to the subway car, proudly bearing the necklace he had recovered.

But he would never know, because as he headed towards the subway, he realized with a start that the train had already left the station and was gone.

"Didn't somebody stop the train while I chased the mugger?" he wondered, confused. "Didn't people see what I was up to? Is it possible the girl doesn't even know I tried to get the necklace for her?"

Tommy was disheartened. Here he had gone to all this trouble, even put his life in danger, and it seemed as if amidst all the tumult, nobody had even realized what he had set out to do.

"Now what?" he wondered.

He decided he would stick around the subway platform in case the girl *had* noticed his heroic efforts, after all, and returned to the station to thank him and find out what happened.

He waited futilely for a full hour, and then concluded that the girl must never even have been aware of his gallant attempts.

"Was all this trouble for nothing?" he wondered, disheartened. "And what do I do with the necklace? The police?" He shook his head. "She doesn't even know someone retrieved it; why would she go to the police? Nah, that's not a good idea . . ."

For some reason that he couldn't quite explain, Tommy decided to hold onto the necklace himself, and keep it with him in his jacket pocket.

And whenever he happened to finger it, as he did from time to time, the vivid recollection of an angelic face with startled sapphire eyes came swimming back to mind.

Three years later, Tommy walked into a bar in midtown Manhattan and there she was. The angelic face and sapphire eyes were unmistakable; he recognized her in an instant. She was perched on a stool near the bar, stirring her drink bemusedly, looking like she was waiting for someone.

"Maybe she's waiting for me," he thought inanely, as his heart lurched.

"This is not a pick-up," he said quickly, as he eased into the stool next to hers. "This is a pick-*me*-up, instead."

"A pick-me-up?" she asked, wrinkling her freckled nose in bewilderment. "Whatever is that supposed to mean?"

"That means," he said, triumphantly pulling out the gold pendant from his pocket where he had kept it all these years, "that when you see this, your spirits will surely be picked up!" And with a theatrical flourish he smugly handed her the necklace, as she stared at him aghast.

As he had correctly discerned in the subway station three years before, amidst the chaos and commotion of the mugging no one—including the girl—had actually seen him dart out the subway door in hot pursuit of the mugger. No one—including the girl—knew that the necklace had been retrieved. And no one could have been more grateful or surprised than she.

"It was my grandmother's," she explained. "Beyond anything else, it has great sentimental value. . . . Tell me," she asked softly, "what can I give you as a reward?"

"How about a date?" Tommy asked.

They've been married for five years now, and Tommy told their story last year on the Valentine's Day program broadcast on a local New York radio station.

In recounting the coincidence that brought them together, Tommy said: "She may have gotten back her necklace, but it was surely *I* who acquired the gem!"

### Comment

Little acts are the seeds from which mighty miracles grow.

*O*lga Whittaker and John Kane, strangers until Tuesday, May 6, 1997, were brought together in a Miami jewelry shop—by fate, coincidence, or was it something else?

Kane, 45, of Fort Lauderdale, was trying to sell a Rolex watch. Whittaker, 36, of West Palm Beach, took a look at the man. She let out a shriek and grabbed him. The jeweler locked the door.

"I prayed to my God that He would kill you, but instead He delivered you into my hands!" Whittaker cried.

The Rolex, she declared, was stolen Sunday from her husband, John K. Whittaker. While running a jewelry booth at an antique show in West Palm Beach, he took the watch off and put it down where he thought it was safe. It was not.

Gone forever, the Whittakers figured, until whatever mysterious wonders were performed Tuesday.

Olga, in Miami for a medical test, went browsing in the Seybold Building, a tall downtown edifice devoted to the jewelry trade.

When the police got there, they found Whittaker, the shopkeeper and a few other people guarding Kane. There was a switchblade knife in his pocket and some open arrest warrants for grand theft on his record, police spokesman Delrish Moss said.

How did Olga Whittaker get him? A miracle, she swears, but she has a police officer's eye for a suspicious character.

"He was at the antique show," she said. "He came to our booth three different times, asking the price of this, the price of that. He looked very pale and nervous then, and the same today."

She also recognized the watch, but needed proof. Her husband brought West Palm Beach Police the papers, which were faxed to Miami, proving that his wife bought that very Rolex for $3,200 in 1990.

Olga Whittaker said she had been praying for a sign that God is real. "This is a big sign," she told Moss.

Kane also spoke to Moss: "Do you know why I was arrested?"

"You tell me," the officer said, hoping for something profound, and the suspect replied, "Bad luck, I guess."

*—Arnold Markowitz*

❧

### Comment

Coincidences are not the result of bad luck, but rather an invitation to look inside and see what might be "bad" that is creating the "luck"!

*Jamey* Martinez and Leslie Duncan were best friends. Even when Leslie switched schools in tenth grade, the two girls stayed close through lots of letters filled with heartfelt confessions and outrageous gossip. Jamey's day always brightened when she saw the familiar blue of Leslie's stationery in her mailbox.

But one crisp fall day, Jamey learned that she would no longer get to share stories with Leslie. A mutual friend broke the incomprehensible news at school: "Jamey, did you hear about Leslie?" Brenda Shwartz, a classmate, asked in a most concerned tone.

"Heard what?" responded Jamey.

Brenda, who had grown up with the two, seemed surprised that Jamey had been in the dark. She stuttered and seemed to falter over her words but then finally she came out with it: "Leslie died last night," she managed to say.

"OK, sure," responded Jamey in a sarcastic tone, "ha, ha, ha."

"No, I'm serious!" Brenda said solemnly.

Jamey knew her friend Brenda very well, and she detected an earnestness in Brenda's voice that told her that she might not be joking after all. Brenda's words were now sinking in.

"No!" screamed Jamey. "No way!" Finding no other words to say, Brenda simply nodded.

Jamey ran back home and got on the phone with Leslie's mother. "Is it true?" she said, trying to choke back emotion. "Is Leslie gone?" There was a long pause as Jamey heard Leslie's mother sobbing on the other end of the line. "Yes," came the choked reply, "Leslie complained that she wasn't feeling good when she came home. She went to sleep and never got up."

Jamey felt that she was swimming in a sea of confusion. The day took on a surreal quality. She wanted to know more; she was unwilling to accept that her friend was gone. Sometime during those hours, Jamey noticed a stack of letters that had come in the mail. There among her parents' bills and correspondence was a familiar blue envelope. A letter from Leslie.

Jamey ripped the letter open with a trembling hand. She hoped it would contain a clue, any information that would shed light on Leslie's mysterious death. But there was no such evidence. It was the usual kind of news. Lots to tell about different classes, things that happened with friends, and places that she had visited.

And, of course, boys. "I want you to meet this guy," the last part of the letter said. "We've been out a couple of . . ." But Jamey stopped reading before the end of the letter. All that seemed trivial now. She folded the letter and placed it with all the other letters from Leslie that she had lovingly saved. The following day she attended her friend's funeral.

Over the next few months, Jamey found solace in making a scrapbook of pictures, letters, and a variety of mementos that helped keep the memory of her deceased friend alive. As the days turned into years and Jamey grew into a woman, she looked at the scrapbook less and less, but she always knew it was there. She had an ache in her heart that was hard to fill. When, in her early twenties, she met a man who filled her with the same kind of joy she had known with her lost friend, she counted her blessings. They got married and moved into a new home.

During the move Jamey came across the scrapbook. Rather than simply putting it away, she opened it. She allowed the contents to take her back in time, smiling at the pictures and reading through some of the letters.

Jamey picked up the last letter she had ever received from Leslie and held it lovingly in her hand. The paper was crumbling a bit, and creased. This time, she read it slowly, to savor the words. And, for the first time, she read the end of the letter that she had skipped ten years ago.

"I want you to meet this guy. We've been out a couple of times," it said. "He's really nice, and you'll like him, I know. I want us all to be friends. His name is Eric Knorr."

As she read the name, her hand flew to her mouth and she let out an audible gasp. The man who filled her heart, the man who shared her home, the man she had married . . . was Eric Knorr.

Leslie's grave is less than a mile from Jamey and Eric's home. The couple visit regularly and lay down a wreath in memory and gratitude, for they believe that their friend's wish played a part in bringing them together.

~ ~ ~

### Comment

Love is the connecting line that links the past, the present, and the future into one everlasting bond that stands the test of time.

*I*n preparation for the onslaught of the Gulf War, when the menacing threat of chemical and biological warfare from Saddam Hussein's factories of death hung over the country of Israel like a dense and sinister fog, Israeli citizens were instructed to create a "sealed" room in their homes to which they could retreat when the Scuds fell.

Almost everyone in Israel understood the grave peril that they faced and the nightmare world into which they had been plunged. They took both Hussein's threats and the worst-case scenario seriously, and in their "sealed" room most Israelis stockpiled abundant supplies of food, medicine, clothing, furniture, books, toys for the children, and additional essentials. Others, however, were more sanguine and consequently didn't equip their room quite as completely as they should have.

The Ben Simone* family belonged to this very small minority. Their sealed room lacked many basics, including furniture. When the first siren went off in Tel Aviv, indicating the beginning of the initial assault, the large family rushed into the sealed room in a state of dazed disbelief. The only piece of furniture in the room was a lone armchair, and practically everyone headed for the floor. Two people remained standing: an elderly grandfather and his young, nine-months-pregnant granddaughter. They both looked at the single armchair and then at each other.

"Grandfather," the young woman urged, "please . . . sit down."

"No, heaven forbid, my sweet, precious grandchild," the elderly man replied. "*You* sit down."

"Not in a million years! I wouldn't think of it! Please, *you* sit down!"

"*I* should sit down while my nine-months-pregnant granddaughter, almost in labor, stands? Never!"

"Well, Grandfather, you might as well sit down, because I absolutely refuse to take *your* chair!"

And so it went, for minutes, a veritable stalemate, both arguing stubbornly, both refusing to yield, the chair remaining empty, unoccupied.

And wasn't it fortunate? Because as they argued, something hit their roof with a loud thud, and a large piece of an unexploded Scud burst through their ceiling and into the armchair where neither of them sat.

ço,ço

### Comment

When we interact with others with love, respect, and consideration, we are enfolded by a protective light.

"**Are** you my father?"

The teenage girl, without preamble or explanation, hurled the question at middle-aged men frantically, as she raced around the cemetery, seemingly possessed.

It was Father's Day, and droves of people were meandering down the labyrinthine burial grounds searching for the graves where they would pay their respects. The atmosphere had been serene and peaceful until the girl had made her frenzied appearance, moments before. Her distraught cries and bizarre behavior unnerved many, and they gazed after her with troubled eyes.

As soon as she had entered the cemetery, the girl had begun waylaying strangers one by one, demanding of each, in breathless tones, if he was her father. As soon as each man shook his head "no"—some pensively, a few annoyed—she would hurry on to accost another.

"Are *you* my father?" she asked, sprinting in a frenzied state from man to man.

"How weird," one woman whispered to her husband.

"Must be on drugs, poor soul," he murmured back.

"Weirdo!" another woman declared, in emphatic tones.

Despite the assured pronouncements of the bystanders, the girl was neither drugged nor crazy.

She had been adopted at birth, and the identity of her biological parents had been kept shrouded in secrecy. But when both of her adoptive parents had died the year before in a tragic car crash, she had launched a desperate search to find her natural mother and father. All that she had learned from the adoption agency was that her natural mother had also died recently and that her biological father's whereabouts were unknown.

But somewhere in the cemetery, a man was waiting. He was leaning up against an old oak tree, eyes scanning the crowd. He was waiting for a teenage girl to approach him and ask, "Are *you* my father?"

He didn't put much stock in dreams, but he had been searching for his daughter for many years without success. And the previous night, a holy man with a luminous face, a long white beard, and piercing eyes had appeared to him in his sleep, with news.

He instructed him to travel to this particular cemetery.

And wait.

A young girl rushed down the path, accosting strangers. His body stiffened. Was it she?

"Are *you* my father?" she asked, desperation tingeing her voice. She had scoured the entire cemetery and was beginning to feel the hopelessness of defeat.

"Are *you* my daughter?" he responded with a tender smile.

"It *is* you, then." She faltered for a moment, gazing with rapt interest into his smoky hazel eyes, replicas of her own.

Later, much later, he asked what had brought her to the cemetery and why she had thought of searching for him there.

"I don't really believe in this kinda stuff," she answered slowly, "but last night a man appeared in my sleep and told me to come to this cemetery today. He said I would find you here for sure. I've been so desperate to locate you, I was ready to try anything. So I did."

"Tell me . . ." the father asked urgently. "What did this man look like?"

"Well, he—umm—kinda had this radiant aura about him, very shiny face, you know? And he had burning eyes. And . . . uh . . . yeah . . . he also wore a long white beard," the daughter said.

"And did he come to you at about two o'clock in the morning?"

"Why, yes," the girl replied, astonished. "I woke up right after the dream—it kinda freaked me out—and looked at the clock on the night table. But . . . how did you know?"

"Honey," the father said softly, "this same man appeared to me last night, too. At the exact same time. Because I also woke up after the dream and looked at my watch. And it was . . . same as you . . . two o'clock.
—*Norman Kelbalkan*

"*D*o you have experience in telecommunications?" Joie Giese inquired of the prospective employee.

"Yes, most certainly," said Merrilee Woeber, trying to put her best foot forward.

"Could you tell me about the places where you have worked and the sorts of jobs you have had?" asked Joie.

Merrilee described her work history, and Joie listened carefully. As supervisor at Network MCI Conferencing, Joie prided herself on creating a dynamic and friendly workforce. In charge of several company projects, she sought to hire men and women of the highest caliber who would add to the positive work ethic that she tried to foster.

So it was without hesitation that Joie decided to hire Merrilee. Intelligent and hard-working, Merrilee fit the job description to a T. Plus, she had a very positive attitude, and Joie found herself extending the interview just because she enjoyed the chat and the pleasant company.

Joie ended the interview with the exact words that Merrilee hoped to hear: "Welcome aboard!"

Merrilee began working for the company almost immediately. The two women became good friends as well as colleagues. They discovered that they had an uncanny similarity in tastes. "I love your outfit," said Joie as she passed Merrilee in the hall one day. "Thanks," came the reply. Several days later it was

Merrilee's turn to offer the compliment. "Now, that's a gorgeous dress," she exclaimed. "Well, thank you," replied Joie. The two found themselves having this sort of exchange repeatedly.

"Look at that," said Merrilee as she placed her ring next to Joie's. Joie was amazed; they both broke into laughter. From the infinite variety of diamond rings available, both women had chosen rings of yellow gold, with identical channel diamonds around the band and a diamond in the center.

One year after being hired, Merrilee was promoted to supervisor. Her desk was now within earshot of Joie's office. Shortly thereafter, Merrilee was working at her desk one afternoon when she overheard Joie chatting with a few coworkers on break. They talked with no particular topic or focus. One woman made a reference to having an Italian complexion. Joie, with her fair skin, made a sarcastic remark. "Yeah, me too," she joked.

Then Joie mentioned in passing something that Merrilee had not known: she had been adopted. Joie said she knew little about her biological parents. Those who knew Joie knew this about her: that she loved her adoptive parents for the abundant love they had given her.

"Do you know your nationality?" the Italian woman asked. "I believe I'm Irish," replied Joie. "The only thing I know about my biological mother is her name. It was Dunne, which is Irish."

It was then that Merrilee stopped typing. Her curiosity got the better of her. She got up and walked right into Joie's office. "I assumed my husband's name when I got married, but my maiden name is Dunne," she said, and then added with a spark of hope, "maybe we're cousins. Where were you born?"

"Here in Davenport," replied Joie.

"That's where I'm from," said Merrilee, eyebrows raised. "When were you born?"

"In 1946," replied Joie.

"I was born in 1945!"

Merrilee and Joie both felt a mounting sense of excitement. They sensed that they were on to something.

"Do you know your biological mother's full name?" asked Merrilee.

"Lenore Dunne," said Joie.

*"NO!"* Merrilee was incredulous. "Are you sure you didn't perhaps just pick up that name from my files?"

"Of course not!" Joie assured her. "That's the name on my adoption papers."

At this point, everyone in the room sensed that something eerie was afoot. One by one, out of courtesy and respect, they filed out. Merrilee and Joie were facing each other alone.

That afternoon, Joie made a dash to her safety deposit box in the bank to retrieve the adoption papers she had received when she turned eighteen. Merrilee, at the same time, looked for a signature from her mother, now deceased. The two women caught up with each other, placed the two signatures side by side, and then simultaneously let out a thrilling cry.

It was unmistakable. No wonder they had so much in common, no wonder they felt an instant connection. They were not only related, they were sisters.

Sisters, born of the same woman — Lenore Dunne. She had had two daughters: one she placed for adoption and one she raised. Each had no knowledge of the other, until now, over half a century later, when they discovered one another while working side by side.

❦

### Comment

To find the greatest of all treasures, you may not need to search the world over.

*D*awn Weiss awoke suddenly in a cold sweat. Secure in her job, safe in her apartment, and surrounded by family and friends, she had no reason to be frightened. Nevertheless, in that early January morning of 1994 the secure world Dawn knew was literally crumbling around her. At first she had a flashback to the days when she was an active alcoholic. Her bed shook and the walls started to crack open. But she was sober now, this was not a hangover, and she knew it. The noise was deafening. What Dawn could not know was that Northridge, California, and its environs were being rocked by an enormous earthquake.

Dawn shot up in bed. Her immediate thoughts were for her beloved Harley, a gray angora cat. "Harley!" she screamed. But the floor was literally swaying beneath her. She had no time to waste as she sprang from her bed. "The whole place is coming down!" she yelled as plaster fell in large chunks from the ceiling. Her natural instincts told her she had no time to save Harley and only seconds to save her own life. She could not even spare a moment to change out of her nightclothes.

She suddenly realized that her second-floor apartment afforded an easy, possibly a simple escape. She ran immediately to the open window. Well within her reach was a large tree branch, which she immediately grabbed.

As the building continued to shake, she lurched for the branch with both hands. Cautiously yet with great trepidation, she groped her way down through the branches to the firm ground below.

The earthquake was relentless as it roared through the area in those dark early-morning hours. It appeared to engulf the terrain around her. As she ran to her car, her apartment building came crashing to the ground like a pile of toy blocks. The parking lot split into a vast crater, swallowing up the cars parked there. The neighbors who had managed to escape stood huddled together, comforting one another yet in shock themselves. Amidst the pandemonium, Dawn spotted Harley the cat. She ran to hug him and held him tight.

In the darkness—through rubble and fallen power lines—holding Harley, Dawn walked for more than a mile to a friend's apartment. Desperately the two of them searched the immediate area for loved ones. Their efforts were not in vain. Within two days Dawn had accounted for all her friends, parents, and other relatives—all, incredibly, alive and uninjured.

For the next two weeks the earthquake's aftershocks made it difficult to trust the earth underfoot. Dawn wanted to believe that the worst was over and that it would never happen again. But then another shock would make the ground tremble. Would it ever cease? After the first week Dawn's nerves were worn thin, leaving her uneasy, uncertain, and anxious about each forthcoming tremor.

"I've got to get out of here, Dad," she told her father. "I can't live like this anymore."

"But, Dawn," pleaded her parents, "everyone you know lives here. We're happy to have you stay with us until you can pull your life together again. Where will you go? What will you do?"

All choked up with many conflicting emotions, Dawn looked at her parents and said simply, "I've got to go. I've just got to get out of this maddening place."

Dawn and her parents paused to reflect. Then gently her father asked again, "Where will you go?"

"I've decided to go to Nashville."

"Tennessee?" asked her father incredulously. "I don't understand that. Do you know anyone there? Why would you choose Nashville?"

Dawn thought for a moment. "I'm not sure, Dad— this whole experience has undone me. I don't feel safe here. I only know that I want to go somewhere— anywhere I'll feel secure. So that's where I'm headed."

Her father was visibly upset. "Dawn," he implored, "you sound just like you did when you were drinking. You don't know anyone in Nashville! Seems to me that this is an irrational choice. You have your network of Alcoholics Anonymous buddies here in California. Dawn, are you relapsing into old behavior? Is this self sabotage?"

"I am not relapsing, Dad," said Dawn. "I've just got to get out of this maddening place and I've chosen Nashville." Her father saw that Dawn would not be dissuaded. He said nothing further about the subject and quietly hoped she would return one day.

Dawn soon learned that her closest friends had also decided to move away from California. Each had found a different place to relocate. With a mixture of sorrow and excitement, Dawn said good-bye to her family and friends, took Harley, and embarked on her tentative journey.

Starting her new life in Nashville, Dawn feared that she would quickly run out of money. She grabbed the first job that was offered to her, as a waitress in a country-style restaurant and bar called Long Horn Steaks. She worked the evening shift so that she could enroll in Middle Tennessee State University. For a number of years she had wanted to earn a degree in mass communications. She now could find the time.

And then, after the third week in Nashville, her past—like the earthquake—came crashing in on her.

The initial excitement of starting her new life had worn off. All of a sudden Dawn looked at her life and was struck by the awesomeness of all that had just transpired. "I can't believe this!" she cried out loud to herself. "The earthquake! All my friends moved away! I'm in a strange new place with new people! All that I have known—everything that's comfortable and familiar—is gone!" She found no solace in her new life. Dawn was struck by a tremendous sense of loss.

In painful self-recognition she turned to God. "I have been sober for three years! I have been so good. Haven't touched a drink all that time. Is this the reward for all my hard work? Must my life spin out of control?" Dawn felt that old familiar urge to drink. She hated it. She was overcome with grief coupled with enormous pain. Having been a member of Alcoholics Anonymous for several years, she knew what she was supposed to do. All she had to do was pick up the phone and call someone for help. She also knew that if she reached out to the Alcoholics Anonymous community, she would find someone with a compassionate ear—someone who would understand and lend as much support as was needed.

Dawn knew all that, but at this moment all she wanted was a bottle to drown her feelings. She longed to submerge herself in some dark haze of oblivion.

Every night, when she should have been focusing on her job, Dawn's thoughts turned more and more to drinking. Alcohol, she felt, would help her blot out a life that was too hard to bear. She watched, almost with envy, the chattering, happy patrons at the bar. It only intensified her desire for a drink.

"That's it," she declared one Friday night on the way to work. "I'm going to have a drink." Dawn figured that there would be more customers than usual at the bar that evening. She could easily blend in unnoticed by others. She entered the restaurant through the back door and proceeded directly to the ladies' room. There she broke down and cried. She was tired of reaching out to new people. She resisted anyone who might understand her plight. Instead she turned once again to God.

"How can you do this?" she found herself repeating. "I sponsored three people who themselves had sponsored others. I volunteered in a women's prison, reaching out to pregnant women and their babies. I came into the program with so much—not like others who come to be sober because they had nowhere else to turn. I was an upstanding, cultured girl. I traveled. I went to the best schools, had loving parents. I had a good job and a car. I'm not supposed to be afflicted with this disease! And this awful life in Nashville is my reward? I'm not even left with a photo album! I have nothing! I feel so abandoned! How much do you think I can endure? I want a drink and now!"

As the door to the ladies' room opened, Dawn quickly wiped away her tears and made sure to muffle her sniffles. Being new at her job, she didn't want to expose herself to anyone. Kim, one of the waitresses, had entered.

"Dawn," she inquired, "who's Bill W.?" Dawn's heart stopped. She was thrown completely off guard by the question. It was the first time she had heard that name since coming to Nashville.

"Bill W.?" Dawn repeated. "He was the founder of Alcoholics Anonymous. Now why would you be asking me that?"

"Haven't you noticed?" Kim replied with some exasperation. "Everyone out there in the restaurant is wearing a pin saying "I AM A FRIEND OF BILL W."

*"What?"* Dawn blurted in total astonishment. She opened the door and surveyed the fifty tables, each filled with an average of five to six people—there must have been close to three hundred people in the restaurant. Sure enough, everyone was wearing a pin declaring his or her allegiance to Alcoholics Anonymous. Then Dawn looked over at Long Horn's popular bar, where she had been planning to have her first drink in three years. It was now completely dark, shut down for the night.

"Oh, my God!" Dawn declared. She approached the first table. "Uh . . . what's going on?"

"Why?" came a voice from the table.

Dawn guessed that no one wanted to break the anonymity of an alcoholic in recovery. "I, too, am a friend of Bill W.," she stated, her voice quivering.

They all sensed her despair. They knew her immediate need. Together they applauded. Then one person spoke up. "We're all here to attend the Alcoholics Anonymous convention. It's our biggest convention ever. Thousands of people from around the world have come to this."

Dawn could hardly believe her ears. Another patron caught her glance. "Yes, we rented out the restaurant for the night, and as for the bartender, we told him that he might as well go home. He was sure to be bored with us."

Dawn sat down at the table. Her fellow A.A. members intuitively understood it all. Intently they listened to her painful story and showered her with love. When she was through, another member spoke up: "What time do you finish work?" she inquired.

"Midnight," answered Dawn.

"What are you doing after work?" the woman asked.

"Well, I was going to drink," said Dawn, "but now . . ." Her words were interrupted. "All six of us were going to the movies after dinner," spoke up another member at the table. "But instead we'll all sit right here until midnight. When you complete your shift we'll all go over to the convention together. There will be twelve step meetings through the night."

"Imagine this," said Dawn with complete gratitude and awe. "Here I was praying for just one person to talk to . . . but God must have thought I was in really rough shape, so he sent me three hundred."

#### Comment

It is possible to be standing on one side of a door and perceive the world as a dark and lonely place, while on the other side of that very same door are countless people just waiting to lend support and cheer you on. All that is required is that you turn the knob.

$\mathcal{T}$*he* call for fire crews came late in the day after dark storm clouds had pitched lightning into the dry grasses, sagebrush and juniper trees covering the deserts of northern Nevada, southern Idaho and Utah. From the Salt Lake Interagency Fire Center frantic calls were made to assemble crews to fight the many fires that had erupted throughout the region.

As I sat on my fire gear in Salt Lake City, waiting for the rest of my crew to arrive, I looked at my hands, callused and swollen from a summer of digging fire lines. It was late July 1994. I was a junior-high-school teacher who spent summers working for the Forest Service. Now, in the hopes of becoming a school social worker, I was scheduled to begin graduate school in the fall. If I were younger, I would have felt more confident. But I wasn't sure I could keep up with the studying. Was I on the right career path?

"Hey, Wright, we're ready to go!" My crew boss, Mike, waved me toward a white bus.

The cargo area in back was already half-filled with shovels, rakes and Pulaskis—tools with an ax on one side and a hoe on the other. As I boarded I put my career concerns aside. The fourteen men and five women on our crew were talking about the fire we were assigned to fight. It was located about 250 miles away in Elko County, Nevada, and had started the day before but had gone unnoticed until that afternoon when winds fanned the flames and enlarged the burned area to thousands of acres.

Just outside of Elko I could see smoke in the distance. We drove up to an old trailer and the bus's air brakes hissed. "A helitack crew has already been flown in and is at work on the mountain about ten miles north of here," the incident commander told us. *Helitack* is a blended word meaning "helicopter attack," when a helicopter crew is flown in to fight a fire. "You're to join them," the commander continued. "Here's the map."

Our bus rumbled on. Pink flags marked our turns, then we pulled up to a makeshift landing pad. As Mike went to get instructions, I sat in the dirt with my back to the hot wind. Soon a faded white helicopter came beating out of the sky toward us. I ducked my head between my knees to keep sagebrush and sand out of my eyes as the copter came down.

"Listen," Mike shouted. "With this wind, the fire is getting bigger fast. They're going to fly us in so we can get right to work. We'll join the helitack crew on top.

"Tim, you're with the first group." By the time I got to the copter, four others were in the back, so I climbed in the seat next to the pilot. As I put on my seat belt harness, I felt the engines gain power and the copter lift. In a few moments we were climbing above the valley and toward the fire.

I watched the skyline apprehensively. A band of ominous dark clouds was getting closer and closer. Along with the drifting smoke, strong winds were kicking up dust below.

Through the haze I saw something moving. Who or what could be down there? Straining my eyes, I saw a pickup truck on the road below, heading for the mountain, following the switchbacks that wound up and around the burning hill. Probably a rancher hoping to save his cattle.

"Ground control—this is Alfa Charlie Seven," the pilot radioed. "Be advised the winds are picking up. The fire's spreading fast." There was a crackling of communication, then another tense exchange. "We've got another problem," the pilot said. "There's a rancher driving up the mountain. Contact him if you can and get him to turn back. With these winds and the way the fire's spreading, he's heading for trouble."

The copter swung high. As the crest of the mountain appeared, the pilot circled, trying to find a place to land. By now we were close enough to see the earlier helitack crew, four people spread out in a line in front of the fire about a mile away from a nearby road. We knew their plan: They would set fire to the area in front of the road, burning it out and creating what is known as a "black." Then, as the main fire roared up to the burnt-out strips, it would run out of fuel and be extinguished.

As the copter dipped toward earth, I fastened my thick, flame-resistant shirt tighter. After many seasons with the Forest Service, I knew what I was in for. In the blazing heat, sticky smoke surges into your face, poisoning the air and stinging your eyes. Green aspens turn to billowing whiteness as leaves, bark and wood dry, then burn with a slow intensity. Goggles and wet bandannas help little. Rocky ground and twisted sagebrush resist blows from the Pulaski, and caulked steel-toed boots grow heavy with sweat. No, I didn't envy those guys on the ground one bit.

I was as ready as I'd ever be. But just as we were about to touch down, the wind gusted and blew the helicopter sideways. The pilot reacted by quickly climbing. The blast continued, swirling black ash into the air.

We rose rapidly to get out of danger. Fed by the sudden winds, the flames had suddenly multiplied, igniting most of the hillside. We watched in horror as the helitack crew, unable to find a way into the "black," began to run from the fury of the fire approaching them.

If the winds diminished and the four firefighters made it through a barbed-wire fence and onto the road, they might have a chance. But where would they go from there? The gap between the firefighters and the flames narrowed. *Run, run!* I thought. The four of them ran for their lives.

I had seen many training films about this sort of situation. We had been instructed to dig an area free of grass and branches and deploy a fire shelter when flames approached and there was no escape. Fire shelters are like small pup tents made of thick fire-resistant cloth with an aluminum coating intended to reflect heat away from the person inside. But there was no time to dig. If the four stopped to take out their fire shelters, they would be incinerated. They continued their desperate run as we watched helplessly from above.

I watched in aching frustration as the four sprinted frantically to reach the dirt road. But with the flames roaring 50 yards behind them and a barbed-wire fence to climb, it seemed impossible.

*"Come on, come on,"* our crew was yelling from the back of the copter. There was no chance of our setting down to help; our pilot was doing all he could to keep the helicopter under control in the fierce gusts. We could only pray, and I did—hard. *I can't see how this is going to work out, God, but maybe you do. Maybe you see something we don't.*

Suddenly out of the swirling blackness it came—the rancher's truck we had seen climbing the other side of the mountain minutes before. He must have seen the running ground crew! Swerving off the dirt road, the truck barreled toward the barbed-wire fence and jerked to a stop alongside it. The rancher jumped out, a pair of wire cutters in his hand. We watched in astonishment as he cut the fence and yanked back the wire.

The rancher leapt back into his truck, waving and yelling at the four to keep running. The flames were almost at their heels as the first firefighter jumped into the back of the truck, then pulled the others in after him.

The flames were around the truck as the last one climbed in. The rancher gunned the engine and took off.

"They made it!" I screamed as the pickup sped down the mountain road. We all cheered with relief while the pilot relayed the news to ground control, then pulled away to land at another site. In a half hour we were on the ground establishing a fire line.

It took more than a week to put out that fire, but I never ran into those guys on the ground and never found out how that rancher happened on those trapped firefighters.

Yet as we watched overhead, two seemingly unrelated scenarios unfolded and came together in a lifesaving rescue. I thought of that dramatic rescue in graduate school as I struggled with my courses and set out to find a new job. Today when I find myself caught with worries about family and work, I remember being high in the sky over Nevada. I think of a fire crew on one side of a mountain frantically trying to outrun a raging firestorm, and a rancher on the other side driving toward what could have been disaster—but what turned out to be a hidden plan.

—*Timothy S. Wright*

#### Comment

Even in the perilous moments of life when all seems to be engulfed in flames, salvation can be but a heartbeat away.

*M*y wife and I were living in Long Beach, California, in the early seventies and I had just gotten a job in the San Francisco Bay area. I was driving my little Volkswagen (we called her Twinky Wilma) up Highway 5, all alone, when it broke down in a desolate and empty expanse of concrete, an isolated and bleak stretch of the freeway. As well as I knew, the nearest gas station or town was more than fifty miles away. My prospects of securing help seemed bleak. I tinkered with the car valiantly, but nothing I tried could get it going again. I finally gave up.

I had been sitting by the side of the road for about an hour, feeling very helpless and forlorn, when I looked at my watch and noted that it was 6:15. Nervously, I wondered if I would get to San Jose in time for my first day of work, 8 A.M. the next morning.

Suddenly, without thinking about it, I automatically reached for the keys and tried to start the engine again. I don't know what prompted me to do that; some inner urge which I could not explain just compelled me to make another attempt. To my stunned surprise, the engine sprang to life as if nothing had ever been wrong with it. What a shock! I got my stuff together, shifted the car into gear and drove the rest of the way without mishap.

That night, I called my wife Kathie to tell her that I had arrived safely in San Jose and that everything was OK.

"Oh," she said, "I wasn't worried. The kids and I prayed for you at dinner tonight. We did a special prayer for Twinky Wilma."

"Do you know what time that was?" I asked.

"Absolutely. I was watching the clock on the stove so dinner wouldn't burn."

"So, what time was it?"

"Six-fifteen exactly."

—*Brad Fregger*

❧

## Comment

When we pray, we are speaking to God. When a miracle happens, God is speaking to us.

*It* was late June and I was living in Philadelphia, where I had lived for nearly a decade, when my employer of six years informed me that after a new corporate structure was put in place on September First my services would no longer be required.

I'm sure this is a scenario familiar to many people and I considered myself more fortunate than most. I was single; I had two months in which to begin my job search while still being employed; and I would be given a six-month severance package. Regardless of this, losing one's job is a very disquieting and distressing event. The initial shock of being laid off soon gave way to emotions wavering somewhere between anger and despair, and although I had the support of my friends and family, I was still left each day with a feeling of isolation.

Over the next two months my job search progressed well. I had already been on several promising interviews and had strong leads on positions in a number of cities: Chicago, Cleveland, New York City, and Washington, D.C. A recruiter based in New York City had even mentioned an opportunity with Hallmark Cards in Kansas City. I had only been in touch with them once or twice, however, and was not considering it as a serious option. Instead my primary focus was on Cleveland, a city within an hour's drive of my family in Youngstown, Ohio. Over the past five years both my brother and sister had moved back to Ohio and I believed, as my parents did, that this job search was the event that would guide my path back home as well.

When you're in the midst of a job search one of the most discouraging times can be the onset of the weekend. For the next two days you hear nothing in response to past inquiries; nothing progresses in the corporate decision making process; and nothing tangible occurs to bring you closer to your goal. For me this was especially disconcerting. I was used to feeling with certainty that I was where I belonged. Even when difficulties arose I always took solace in the notion that this was the right direction, this was my path, and if I stuck with it long enough, things would be resolved. I had come to rely on the strength that assurance gave me, but now that inner support was gone. I was adrift with no clear direction.

One Friday evening in late August, feeling especially disheartened by the events in my life, I walked to a local pizzeria to order a sandwich. It was a shop I was familiar with, and after placing my order, I walked to the front window to watch the last of the daily commuters file from the train station to make their way home for the weekend. I felt melancholy.

What depressed me was not the work involved in my job search—I enjoyed the challenge and things continued to progress well—rather it was the uncertainty of where my life was headed.

Although I would not consider myself a religious person (not having attended church on a regular basis since childhood), I have always considered myself to be very spiritual. The nature of my relationship with God is more a dialogue than ritualistic reverence. That night, standing by the window, I asked God for a sign, anything that would give me an idea of what my future held and where my path would lead.

I turned from the window telling myself there was nothing to be done, it was the weekend and I should try to relax. At the same time I became aware of the television that the owners had installed on a shelf in the corner above the window to watch, among other things, the game show *Jeopardy*. As my anxiety began to abate, my mind became attuned to the show, and the first question I clearly recall the host asking dealt with naming the company that began marketing a small line of Collectible Ornaments in 1973. While one contestant answered incorrectly, another responded, "What is *Hallmark?*" to which the host replied, *"Hallmark is the correct answer."*

At first I couldn't believe what I had just heard. I turned toward the television and was even more surprised to find that the contestant who had answered the question correctly was named Matt. That's my name, I thought. How strange.

My job search would take many twists and turns over the following two months, and regardless of the sign I had been given that night at the pizza shop, I had resigned myself to believe that I would either stay in Philadelphia or move back closer to my family in Ohio. Neither was meant to be. Offers that I felt confident were forthcoming never materialized, while others were clearly not the right choice. All the while I could feel a gentle but firm hand pushing me in a new direction, toward Kansas City, where I now live, and Hallmark Cards, where I've been gainfully employed since early last December.

—*Matt Eichmann*

*L*ife's *a little thing!* Robert Browning once wrote. But a little thing can mean a life. Even two lives. How well I remember. Two years ago in downtown Denver my friend, Scott Reasoner, and I saw something tiny and insignificant change the world, but no one else even seemed to notice.

It was one of those beautiful Denver days. Crystal clear, no humidity, not a cloud in the sky. We decided to walk the ten blocks to an outdoor restaurant rather than take the shuttle bus that runs up and down the Sixteenth Street Mall. The restaurant, in the shape of a baseball diamond, was called The Blake Street Baseball Club. The tables were set appropriately on the grass infield. Many colorful pennants and flags hung limply overhead.

As we sat outside, the sun continued to beat down on us, and it became increasingly hot. There wasn't a hint of a breeze, and heat radiated up from the tabletop. Nothing moved, except the waiters, of course. And they didn't move very fast, either.

After lunch Scott and I started to walk back up the mall. We both noticed a mother and her young daughter walking out of a card shop toward the street. She was holding her daughter by the hand while reading a greeting card. It was immediately apparent to us that she was so engrossed in the card that she did not notice a shuttle bus moving toward her at a good clip. She and her daughter were one step away from disaster when

Scott started to yell. He hadn't even gotten a word out when a breeze blew the card out of her hand and over her shoulder. She spun around and grabbed at the card, nearly knocking her daughter over. By the time she picked up the card from the ground and turned back around to cross the street, the shuttle bus had whizzed by her. She never even knew what almost happened.

To this day two things continue to perplex me about this event. Where did that one spurt of wind come from to blow the card out of that young mother's hand? There had not been a whisper of wind at lunch or during our long walk back up the mall. Secondly, if Scott had been able to get his words out, the young mother might have looked up at us as they continued to walk into the bus. It was the wind that made her turn back to the card—in the one direction that saved her life and that of her daughter. The passing bus did not create the wind. On the contrary, the wind came from the opposite direction.

I have no doubt it was a breath from God protecting them both. But the awesomeness of this miracle is that she never knew. As we continued back to work, I wondered how God often acts in our lives without our being aware. The difference between life and death can very well be a little thing.

❦

Comment
Miracles often blow unseen through our lives.

*E*ditor Arnold Fine of the *Jewish Press* once received an unusual letter from an elderly reader. "I faithfully read and enjoy your column 'I Remember When,' and am often struck by the warmth and sensitivity of your writing. You seem like a person who really cares, which is why I am turning to you for help.

"Although I am now eighty years old and a widow, I cannot forget my first love, Harry. I was seventeen and quite sure—at my tender age—that I had already found my soul mate. Harry, a mature twenty-three, was also convinced that we were fated for each other and that his quest for his life's partner was also over. We were madly, passionately, unrestrainedly in love.

"But my parents didn't share my enthusiasm for Harry. They were bitterly opposed to the relationship not so much because of our youth—although it was a factor—but because Harry was from the 'wrong side of the tracks.' My parents were wealthy, influential, fourth-generation American-Germans; Harry's were indigent and newly arrived Eastern European immigrants. Consequently, my parents did everything in their power to sabotage the match.

"They were so alarmed about the possibility of my marrying Harry, in fact, that they took me to Europe for a year. When I returned, Harry seemed to have disappeared from the face of this earth. He had moved, and had left no forwarding address. No one seemed to know his whereabouts. I tried desperately to find him, but never succeeded. I was heartbroken. I would never love anyone again the way I had loved Harry.

"A few years later, I married a wonderful man with whom I lived happily for almost sixty years and we did have a very good life together. He died last year.

"I guess I have a lot of time on my hands now, but lately I just can't seem to get Harry out of my mind. I constantly wonder what happened to him, and if he's still alive. I know it's a long shot, but I thought if anyone could help me, it would be you, Mr. Fine. I know you are a busy man, but if you could possibly help me try to trace Harry, I would be eternally grateful.

"The only clue I can provide is this ancient envelope with Harry's old address which I am enclosing. I now live in the Crown Manor Nursing Home* in Long Beach, where I await with faith and yearning, your answer."

The letter was signed Ida Brown.*

Arnold Fine was indeed a busy man. In addition to his editorial duties at the *Jewish Press*, he worked during the day as a special education teacher in the New York City public school system.

But the letter had moved him, and he vowed to help Ida. Using all the investigative expertise that he had acquired from years working as a newspaper reporter, he set out to find Harry. He embarked on the project with both hope and trepidation. He would be deeply gratified if he could indeed locate Harry and reunite the two. But what of the other possibility? What if he had to report to Ida that Harry was long dead?

Several weeks later, Arnold Fine journeyed to the Crown Manor Nursing Home* for a very special occasion. First, he went to the sixth floor, where he shook hands with an elderly but chivalrous-looking gentleman, alert and vital, eyes snapping with wit and energy despite the cane at his side. Arnold draped his arm gently around his shoulders and carefully guided him into the elevator, which they took to the third floor where Ida was waiting.

"Harry?" trembled Ida as she stood looking at him from across the hall.

"My God . . . Ida!" he stammered.

Unbeknownst to one another, the two had been living in the same nursing home for five months, three floors apart.

Several weeks later, Arnold Fine traveled to the Crown Manor Nursing Home a second time. This time, he had come to attend Ida and Harry's wedding, some sixty years in the making.

༄

### Comment
The heart that loves does not forget. Its passion is like a burning flame that is kept alive by memory.

*Early* one morning, Pat was rudely awakened out of a deep slumber by the shrill ringing of the telephone. Groggily, she raised her eyes to the digital clock on the night table and was astonished to see that it was only 5 A.M.

"This better be good," she thought.

It was an obscene phone call.

She slammed down the phone angrily and tried pulling the covers over her head, willing herself back to sleep.

But she couldn't exorcise the man's foul language or lewd suggestions from her head.

"Maybe it's not such a good idea for me to live alone," she thought.

She tossed and turned in bed, but it was useless, really. She couldn't get back to sleep. Her nerves were jangled from the call. Under her breath, she cursed the caller over and over again.

"Better get up and make yourself a strong cup of coffee," she advised herself.

She stumbled into the kitchen, still cursing the caller, God, life, the universe, fate, and anyone else she could think of for disrupting her sound night's sleep.

But her perspective changed the moment she turned on the overhead light. Her kitchen window, which she had firmly closed the night before, was now wide open. And a wicked-looking butcher's knife that she did not own lay on the kitchen table, together with a ski mask and a rope.

When Pat absorbed the significance of the open window and the malevolence of the items on her kitchen table, she gasped.

What had happened or was about to happen to her was clear.

An intruder had slipped into her apartment, preparing an attack.

And at that precise moment, the telephone must have rung.

Scaring her out of her mind.

And scaring the attacker out of her apartment.

*"Thank you, God,"* she murmured. "And thank you, Mr. Obscene Phone Caller," she added. "I was disgusted by your call, but apparently it saved my life."

❧

### Comment

One can never be sure when to laugh or when to cry. When to curse or when to bless. For life often speaks to us in cryptic signs and we can't be sure of the final picture until all the pieces of the puzzle fall into place.

*It* was in the middle of a blizzard, and my brother was trying to get home from work. After waiting an hour for a bus, he decided to try to walk home. The snow was very high and walking was very difficult, but he kept at it. After what seemed like a lifetime he was nearly home. It was a good thing too, because he was freezing and didn't think he could last much longer.

Just then his foot hit something and to his horror, he realized that a woman was lying in the snow. At first he wasn't sure that the woman was alive, but as he knelt down he heard her moan. She said that she too had been trying to walk home but she fell and wasn't able to get up. My brother didn't know what to do. He could hardly drag himself along, but he made a tremendous effort and picked her up.

Somehow he got her into a building next door where she sat and warmed up. They exchanged names and addresses and when he was sure that she would be able to make it home, my brother left her and walked the remaining three blocks to his apartment.

My brother didn't make too much of this incident. He thought he had just done what anyone else would have done, but to us he was a real hero.

Imagine his surprise when the following week in the same envelope as his paycheck, there was a check for $5,000 and a note from his boss thanking him for *saving his sister's life!*

"*Chronic* renal failure," doctors told my cousin Larry, hooked up to dialysis machines for more than four years but deteriorating rapidly. "Your only hope is a kidney transplant." I, among several other relatives, was asked to give samples to see if a compatible donor could be found. I readily agreed, without contemplating the consequences. It came as a shock to learn that I was the perfect match.

The call came from the hospital in the middle of my four-year-old daughter's birthday party. My wife, eight months pregnant with our second child, threw me a wary look when I hung up the phone. She had caught the nuances of the muted conversation, my careful responses. I hadn't wanted to spoil the party, for her sake or my daughter's. "What is it?" she asked. "Not now," I said, looking pointedly at our child and the birthday cake.

"This is really *big*, Ronnie," she said, distressed, when our daughter fell asleep later that evening and we withdrew to the kitchen to talk. "Can we think about this for a while?"

"He doesn't have much time, Debra. I told the doctors I would give them an answer tomorrow."

"*Tomorrow?*" she shrieked, furious. "What do you think . . . the kidney is an extra tire? What happens when you need a spare? Will someone be around to give *you* one?"

"Debra," I said, "this isn't easy for me, either. Believe me, I'm absolutely terrified! And I'm torn and ambivalent. If I'm really honest with myself, I have to admit I would have been vastly relieved to find out I *wasn't* a match. But the fact is that I am."

"Ronnie," Debra said firmly, "this is a *major* surgery, with serious risks involved. I forbid you to go through with it!"

"Larry is like a brother to me, Deb. It's not something I *want* to do; it's something I *have* to do. What's my life going to be worth if I deny Larry the right to live?"

"This is a *major* decision, Ronnie, one that involves *all* of us. You have a family now, and a responsibility to this family, too!"

"Debra," I said weakly, "I have to sleep on this."

"I don't want you to do this . . . Ronnie, I just can't allow you to take the risk!" And she stormed out of the room, her eyes ice cold, her chin set in determination.

Part of me longed to cave in to her demands and accede. I could blame it on her . . . "So, sorry, Larry, but as you know Debra's about to give birth and she just won't allow me to . . ." I envisioned myself saying. But another part of me repudiated that scenario, ashamed.

That night, I tossed and turned in bed in a restless slumber, agonizing over what to do. And then I had a dream.

In the dream, I was visiting Larry at the hospital.

I walked in, arranging a cheerful face prior to my entry, and called out in an insincere, hearty manner: "Hey, buddy, how's life?"

"*This* is *not* life," Larry answered bitterly. "Can't eat food . . . barely allowed to drink . . . hooked up to the machine for hours, and when the hellish procedure is over, I feel worse than ever."

"But Lar," I interjected, still attempting false cheer. "At least, this procedure lets you move and you're free!"

"Yeah, free!" he replied sourly. "Free to go *to* dialysis and *from* dialysis." He motioned toward the wires hooking him up to the machine. "I'm twenty-eight years old and I've got an umbilical cord that's like a ball and chain!"

"Larry," I said helplessly, "what can I do?"

"I can't go on like this anymore. Help me, please!" he cried.

I woke up in a cold sweat.

And I resolved—despite my wife's anger and my own misgivings—to give him my kidney.

As I was wheeled into the operating room, the doctor at my side murmured encouragement. "You're in good hands, Ronnie," he said. "You've made a decision you can live with."

The next morning, I woke up groggy and saw a doctor hovering near my side. "Good morning, Ronnie!" he said cheerfully. "How are you feeling . . . aside from the normal postoperative discomfort?" he asked.

"Doc," I groaned, "I don't know what normal is, but I sure am in a lot of pain."

"Yes . . . well . . ." He hesitated for a fraction of a second. "I must tell you that something we were not prepared for occurred during the operation . . ."

"What's happened to Larry?" I asked, alarmed.

"He's still on dialysis, but don't worry, we have another match all lined up for him."

I stared at the doctor, confused.

"Ronnie," he began gently, "I doubt that you have ever heard of *renal cell carcinoma?*" I shook my head no. "It's an incurable form of cancer," he continued, "virtually always fatal."

"Are you saying that Larry has . . ." I asked tremulously, my heart palpitating, even as the doctor interrupted me in mid-sentence.

"No, Ronnie, he was spared. . . . And so were you. Your ultrasound indicated two healthy kidneys, Ronnie. Either one of them would have saved your cousin. And it was arbitrary . . . or so we thought . . . which one we chose to remove. Little did we know that our hands were being guided to the correct one. . . . Because, Ronnie, once we removed your left kidney, the naked eye was able to see what the ultrasound had failed to show. On the left kidney cortex was a tiny nodule, a nodule of renal cell carcinoma. Had you not elected to donate your kidney to your cousin, you could easily have been dead within a year. And had the kidney not been inspected as thoroughly as it was, Larry would have been dead from *your* cancer. . . . Ronnie, your intentions were indeed very noble. You thought you were saving your cousin's life—but as it turns out, my friend, it was Larry who saved *yours*."

❧

### Comment

The universe repays kindness, not measure for measure, as humans do, but with infinite generosity and grace.

*P*erhaps God didn't talk to me through my dog.

Perhaps it just seemed that way—not just to me, but to a friend who witnessed the event. But considering that God—the Judeo-Christian God, at least—has employed burning bushes and ghostly images of the Virgin to communicate with mortals, maybe my lop-eared, Roman-nosed coon hound wasn't such an outlandish choice for a conduit between the mundane and the ethereal.

In any case, the events happened as described. And if what follows wasn't the result of an unseen hand attempting to turn me from my casual agnosticism, it was at least a truly paranormal incident, the only one I've ever experienced.

The time: a few years ago. I was renting a small cabin on the grape ranch my friend David Steiner owned and operated on Sonoma Mountain. One spring day, we decided to go salmon fishing the following morning. And because we're both susceptible to seasickness, we stuck scopolamine skin patches behind our ears before retiring for the night. Scopolamine has some undesirable side-effects—cotton mouth, ringing ears and a sense that roaches are crawling across your skin—but for me, there's no substitute.

The alarm woke me at 3 the next morning. With swollen eyes and parched throat, I dressed and shuffled across the compound to Steiner's house. He was already up, looking as rocky as I felt, dolefully watching his Mr. Coffee fill a pot with viscous, black brew. We drank a couple of cups each and started making sandwiches and collecting our gear: rods, tackle, rubber boots, sweatshirts. It took about a half hour before my truck was loaded and we were ready to go.

My head, sinuses and throat felt like they were packed with wool and cockleburs. The scopolamine was in high gear. I felt like hell, but at least I wouldn't spend the whole day clutching the rail.

Somehow, though, I sensed I had forgotten something. Fishing license? I checked: it was in my wallet. Something still disturbed me, but I didn't have time to dwell on it. We faced an hour drive to Bodega Bay, and the boat left at 5 o'clock—no time to dither. We took off.

From the ranch, Sonoma Mountain Road snakes down a hill for a half mile. Well before we reached the bottom, my vague unease changed to epiphany: the sodas. Or the Pepsi Lights, more accurately—a six-pack of Steiner's favorite nonalcoholic beverage. We had left them in his refrigerator, and it was unthinkable that we could proceed without them. The prospect of that icy, caffeinated, artificially sweetened nectar trickling down my ravaged throat was too much to resist: I had to have one immediately.

"What's the deal?" grumbled Steiner.

"Pepsis," I rasped. "We forgot 'em."

But as I looked for a driveway to use as a turnaround, my headlights illuminated the eyes of a large animal in the road. It was proceeding toward us with an oddly spavined gait, one I recognized immediately. Megan. The dire hound.

Did I own Megan? No, hounds are the most feline of dogs. She deigned to stay around the place as long as I fed her regularly and granted her access to the compost pile. One of her favorite pastimes was patrolling the road in front of the ranch for road kill. I tied her up or kept her fenced as much as possible, but she found ways to graze the asphalt when my back was turned or I was preoccupied—as I was that morning, with a throbbing skull of scopolamine.

I was irritated to see Megan. She endangered herself by her presence on the road and dealing with her would delay us. We could literally miss the boat.

I downshifted, and she stopped in the middle of the pavement, recognizing the sound of the truck's engine. I could see she had something in her mouth, and I pulled up next to her, opening the door. "Give me that, Megan," I said, grabbing her booty.

It was a six-pack of icy cans. I held them up to the windshield, so we could see what they were. Pepsi Lights, so cold they were rimmed with frost. We knew without checking they weren't the colas from Steiner's fridge. (We looked when we got home; the sodas were still there.)

I could feel the hair stand up on the back of my neck.

I looked down at Megan, who gazed up at me with her blank, vaguely expectant expression.

"Megan," I said. "Bad dog. Go home." She skulked away into the blackness. Steiner popped the top of one of the cans and took a swig. I followed suit. The Pepsi was balm to my throat, exactly what I needed at that moment. We sat for a minute in the dark, spinning through possible scenarios. Had she found an ice chest in the road? Did some friendly passerby give her a six-pack, thinking her a thirsty hound in need of hydration? Had she broken into a neighbor's house, jimmied the refrigerator, padded out with the Pepsi Lights, ignoring sausages, cheese, leftover pot roast?

Or was some higher power involved? How could this happen at the precise moment Steiner and I were discussing not mere beverages, not generic soft drinks — but Pepsi Lights? Was this some kind of a sign??

Such synchronicity of time and events seemed impossible unless a divine intelligence — albeit one with a sense of humor — had chosen to tweak the cosmic clockwork.

"I know this must mean something," Steiner said, "but I'll be damned if I can figure out what it is."

We went fishing and caught nothing all day. The skies were gray, the ambient temperature was low and the seas were high. Despite the scopolamine, Steiner got seasick and spent a considerable portion of his time hanging over the side. I felt queasy, but managed to keep everything down. The colas helped.

I've been importuned by people peddling spiritual nostrums all my life. Neighborhood preachers, evangelical fire-breathers, Hare Krishnites, Jehovah's Witnesses, New Age gurus, crystal hawkers—I've been immune to them all. None offered what I needed most: proof. Only my dog could do that. She's dead now, laid six feet deep at the roots of a gnarled pear tree on the ranch—gone, perhaps, to that great, reeking compost pile in the sky. I could not have entertained the prospect that a heaven existed for either humans or dogs before we saw Megan jackknifed in the middle of the road, a six-pack depending from her maw. Now I'm not so sure. Now I think there may be something—out there. Beyond. After. Something.

Megan: Go Home.

—*Glen Martin*

*O*n a sun-splattered June day in 1991, Cantor Michael Weisser and his wife Julie were enjoying a leisurely Sunday brunch in their new home in Lincoln, Nebraska, when the telephone rang. Outside, birds chirped harmoniously and children's sweet voices wafted into the air; from inside the modest, two-bedroom brick ranch came the buoyant sounds of laughter and cheer, as Julie, her close friend Rita Babbitz, and Michael traded quips in an atmosphere of comfort and camaraderie. The telephone had been ringing all morning long; the Weissers were a popular couple in Lincoln, and, as spiritual leader of one of the city's two synagogues, Michael was plied with questions and appeals continuously. There was no reason for him to feel apprehensive as he reached for the phone; no cause for him to suspect that the caller was anyone other than a well-wisher or a congregant. So it was in a spirit of complete ease that Michael crossed the room to answer the phone's insistent ring, unaware that with this simple act the peace and tranquillity of the Weisser household was about to be shattered for a long time to come.

"You will be sorry you ever moved into 5810 Randolph Street, Jew boy," a man's voice—harsh and dripping with menace—rasped. Then the phone went dead.

Michael Weisser had previously served in synagogues in Tennessee, California, Ohio, Florida, and

South Carolina—some of these pulpits in towns with minuscule Jewish populations—and although he had encountered subtle forms of bigotry in many of these places, he had never received a hate call before.

From across the room, Julie Weisser observed her husband's pained expression and, more ominously, his silence.

"What's the matter?" she asked.

Michael repeated the warning message and, trembling with anger, said: "I bet it's the Klan."

"I don't think it's the Klan," said his son Dave, who had happened to pick up the extension in his room upstairs and had heard the warning too. "It's probably just some crackpot."

"A crackpot from the Klan," Michael insisted.

He was right.

On the southwest side of Lincoln, a bearded man laughed hoarsely as he slammed down the phone. He was wearing a gold swastika on a chain around his neck and a faded red T-shirt with the words "White Power" printed in white next to a black swastika. Blue-gray tattoos—a skull and crossbones with "Hell's Angels" written underneath, a heart pierced by an arrow and an Iron Cross, a German military symbol used as a Nazi emblem—adorned his arms. Nazi rings with swastikas glittered on his fingers.

His name was Larry Trapp and his official title was "Grand Dragon of the White Knights of the Ku Klux

Klan for the Realm of Nebraska." His job was spreading hatred throughout the state, and although he was a double amputee confined to a wheelchair, he worked frenetically every day to fulfill his mission. He hated Jews, African Americans, Asians, Mexicans, and Indians. He enjoyed violence, and he particularly liked to scare blacks and Jews. His ugly call to Michael Weisser was just the beginning of a campaign of harassment he planned against the cantor and his wife.

Cantor Weisser was a man fervently dedicated to promulgating the principles of love, tolerance, and nonharmful behavior—three basic ideas he perceived to be at the heart of the Jewish faith. During his first sermon at Lincoln's Bnai Jeshurun Synagogue, Michael had passionately declared: "In Jewish tradition, our role as human beings is to correct the universe. So how do we do that? We look at the things that we have done to place barriers between human beings and the rest of natural creation. Little by little, we need to tear down those barriers and make them disappear so we can experience the fullness of each other and the richness of the creation, which is given to us as a gift and of which we are a part."

Two days after the menacing phone call, Julie Weisser found a thick brown manila envelope in her mailbox, addressed in capital block letters to "RABBI MICHAEL WEISSER." Inside was anti-Semitic literature—flyers, brochures, and horrible, racist cartoons. On top of the stack of material was a card that read: "The KKK is watching you, scum." Other handwritten messages warned: "The 'Holohoax' was nothing compared to what's going to happen to you!"; "Heil Hitler! May his memory refresh your soul and give you inspiration!"; "Your Time is Up"; and "Those responsible for the suffering of our White Race (Jews, Blacks, Race-Mixers, and Whites who support them) will pay the penalty for High Treason with Death by Hanging." The second phase of Larry Trapp's campaign of harassment against the Weissers had been implemented, with a vengeance.

But the Weissers were not the sole focus nor the only target of Larry Trapp's malevolence. He preyed on African Americans and Asians continuously; homes owned by members of these ethnic groups were firebombed, hate literature was strewn across their steps. As part of an ongoing hate campaign that the Grand Dragon labeled "Operation Gooks," a Vietnamese social welfare center was trashed, the furniture inside hacked to pieces, electrical wires ripped from the walls, water pipes broken—the heinous destruction obliterating the center out of existence. Trapp installed a telephone hot line that spewed messages of hate; one particular tape singled out a black woman named Donna Polk whom he had terrorized for months. On this tape, he announced her address with the intimation that she was fair game for hunters seeking good quarry. He convinced the local public access channel to air "Race and Reason," a despicable paean to the White Aryan Resistance Movement.

Michael Weisser was one of those who watched the revolting show, and his horror at the hatred and destruction Trapp had unleashed in Lincoln surged throughout his being like a powerful current. Not only had he and his wife been victimized by the man, but countless others had been swept up by the tide of vitriol coursing through the city. All his life, Michael had challenged, confronted, and acted on his anger. He picked up the phone and called Trapp.

But Trapp didn't answer. Instead, Weisser heard the newest edition of the Grand Dragon's hot line: "Vigilante Voices of Nebraska—where the truth hurts!" The message on this tape was so malignant that Michael could no longer contain his fury. He waited for the beep and said: "Larry, you better think about all this hatred you're spreading, because one day you're going to have to answer to God for all this hatred, and it's not going to be easy."

From that time forward, Michael Weisser began to habitually leave little messages on Larry Trapp's tape. They were impulsive, never prepared or prerehearsed. Michael just said whatever came into his mind. Something in him was compelling him to talk to the Grand Dragon, even though he couldn't know whether he was being heard or understood at all.

Once, after Larry Trapp appeared on a local television program dressed in full Klan regalia standing beneath a Nazi flag, Michael reached for the phone and left another message for Larry.

"I just saw the interview in which you stood so proudly near a Nazi flag," Michael said. "Larry, do you know that the very first laws that Hitler's Nazis passed were against people like yourself who had no legs or who had physical deformities, physical handicaps? Do you realize you would have been among the first to die under Hitler? Why do you love Nazis so much?"

Larry Trapp listened to the message, as he had to all the other messages Michael Weisser had repeatedly left over the last several weeks. The others he had dismissed and scorned, but this one hit home. He knew that Michael's words were true. The Nazis *had* exterminated the physically handicapped, even before they began to gas the Jews.

"What will I do if Trapp ever picks up the phone?" Michael asked Julie one day after he had left a message on Trapp's machine that urged: "How can you feel any real sense of freedom when you're doing all these hateful things? Maybe you should let all that hate go."

Julie had thought about Trapp and his hate-filled existence many times. She had often wondered what terrible circumstances must have wrought such hatred, and had concluded that Trapp must have been sorely deprived of love when he was young.

"If he ever answers the phone, tell him you want to do something nice for him," she said. "Tell him you'll take him to the grocery store or something like that. It'll totally freak him out."

Michael loved Julie's idea and wondered whether he would have the opportunity to implement it. Trapp had never picked up his phone when Michael called. "Had his calls made the slightest dent?" Michael wondered time and time again.

Trapp hated the calls. They were beginning to get under his skin. He had to stop them; he had to stop the man whose warm voice with its undertones of laughter broadcast messages of love into his room. "He's some crackpot," he told another Klansman one day when Michael's voice, coming over the tape machine, exhorted: "Larry, when you give up hating, a whole world of love is waiting for you." "The next time he calls, I'll answer, and put a stop to this harassment once and for all," Larry vowed.

When the call came, Larry was ready.

"What the —— d'ya want?" he growled.

Michael followed Julie's directive. "Well, I was thinking you might need a hand at something," he said. "And I wondered if I could help. I know you're in a wheelchair and I thought maybe I could take you to the grocery store or something."

For several long seconds, Trapp didn't speak. His shock was palpable, even over the telephone wires.

Finally, he coughed and began to speak. Michael fancied that Trapp's voice sounded different than before, less brittle, softer, almost as if the hatred that had laced it before had suddenly, miraculously disappeared.

"That's OK," Larry Trapp said. "That's nice of you, but I've got that covered. Thanks, anyway. But don't call this number anymore. It's my business phone."

"I'll stay in touch," Michael Weisser said quickly before Trapp could hang up the phone.

On Friday night, November 15, 1991, Michael Weisser delivered a Sabbath sermon that electrified his congregation with its warm messages of benevolence, charity, and humanitarianism.

"If we don't communicate our love through the work of our hands, then what kind of love do we have?" he said. "Love means being willing to aid and serve the one who is unloved. And if we keep our tolerance to ourselves, it is not really tolerance at all, but merely silence. In order to express our tolerance, we are called to reach out to those who may seem different—reach out and make them our friends."

Following the sermon, it was traditional for the congregation to engage in a silent prayer for friends and family who were ill. Michael had already stepped down from the dais, when Larry Trapp's image sprang to mind. Impulsively, Michael turned to his congregation and asked them to pray for someone who was sick—not physically sick in the ordinary sense, but "sick from the illness of bigotry and hatred. Please pray that he be healed, too."

That Friday night, as prayers were being said for him, Larry Trapp's sleep was fitful and restive. The swastika ring on his left hand and the swastika ring on his right hand began to feel, for the first time in his life, heavy and uncomfortable. For some odd reason, his ring fingers began to burn, itch, and sting. This had never happened before. He took the rings off because they seemed to hurt his fingers. When his fingers felt better, he put the rings back on. When they started bothering him again, he took them off. He was frightened by what was happening; some thick, impending presence seemed to hang in the air.

All night long, Larry Trapp took the rings off, put them back on, and then took them off again—and couldn't understand why.

The next evening, he called Michael Weisser. "I want to get out," he said, "but I don't know how."

"Would you like some help?"

"I don't know. I don't think so."

"Well, maybe we could talk about this tonight."

"I don't think so. Maybe later sometime."

"Look," Michael said. "Are you hungry? My wife and I'll get some food and come over and bring you dinner."

"Well, I don't know . . ."

"We can have some food and break some bread together."

"Well, OK, I guess that would be all right."

Michael and Julie were inside the car, fastening their seat belts, when Julie had a thought.

"Wait a second, Michael. I think we should bring Larry some kind of gift to show him we're sincere. Let me run into the house and see what I can find."

But once inside the house, Julie was at a loss as to what to bring. "Can't bring a book," she mused out loud, "he's blind. Can't bring sweets—he's a diabetic. Can't bring clothing—don't know what size he wears." She walked into her bedroom, began looking through a little brass jewelry box on the dresser, and saw the perfect gift.

It was a silver ring of intertwined strands she had bought for Michael two years ago. Michael had liked it, but rarely wore it. "It's exactly what I want to give Larry!" she thought with growing excitement.

"Don't you think this ring is perfect?" she asked Michael, returning to the car with her prize. "I like it because it's all twisted up, but it's very beautiful. To me it symbolizes how somebody's life can be all twisted up but still turn out beautifully in the end."

"That's an interesting perspective," Michael responded. "I never looked at the ring quite that way."

"*I've* always thought of it as a brotherhood ring. To me, those strands represent all the different kinds of people on this earth, different, but nonetheless, very much intertwined."

Larry Trapp extended his hand when he opened the door for Michael and Julie. "Hi there," he said.

"It's good to meet you in person," Michael said, warmly clasping Larry's outstretched hand.

At the touch of Michael's hand, Larry winced. He felt as if he had been hit by a jolt of electricity. Then he broke into tears.

Larry didn't know what impulse compelled him, but he suddenly began yanking at the two silver swastika rings on his fingers. "I can't wear these anymore," he cried. "They stand for all the hatred in my life. Will you take them away?"

Michael and Julie stared at each other in shock, stunned by the coincidence. "We will take them away and give you a new one instead," Michael murmured softly.

"Here," said Julie, gently sliding the new ring onto Larry's finger. "We want you to have this. I feel the strands symbolize the beauty of a person's soul, and Michael feels they stand for brotherhood. But one thing is certain. Surely, this ring stands for love."

And then all three clasped hands together and cried.

*Epilogue:* Larry Trapp resigned his position with the Ku Klux Klan, renounced his membership in all the hate organizations he had joined, and made amends to the people in Lincoln, Nebraska, whom he had harassed over the years. He called each one of them individually and asked for forgiveness. He met with law enforcement officials from various agencies such as the FBI, the Anti-Defamation League, and the local police and gave them inside information on the activities of hate organizations operating underground in the United States. He converted to Judaism on June 5, 1992, and died three months later of diabetic-related illness. During the last several months of his illness, he had moved in with the Weissers, who nursed him tenderly until his death.

# *Acknowledgments*

Our thanks go first and foremost to YOU, our cherished readers, whose enthusiasm for the message of our first book has been boundless and immensely gratifying. Because of *your* warmth and excitement we have been able to proceed with this second book. We have been enormously moved by your kind and sincere letters and are very heartened to know that *Small Miracles* has brought you joy and comfort. *You* our readers are the co-creators of this sequel, and we applaud you for your open hearts and contagious excitement.

Our deep gratitude also goes to everyone at Adams Media, who launched this book with so much trust, belief, and devotion. To the extraordinary Bob Adams, who took such enormous personal interest in the fate of this small book and expended so much creative energy in launching it, who believed in the book even more after he experienced his own first "small miracle" the very night he finished reading the galleys. To Wayne Jackson, innovative and dynamic Director of Marketing, whose zeal for the book was contagious and set booksellers on fire. Thanks also to Melanie Mackinaw for her special efforts and gracious assistance in all spheres of publicity support.

We have been blessed with the most wonderful editor, Pamela Liflander, whose expert advice, gentle wisdom, and intelligent counsel have greatly enriched our writing experience. We have concluded that Pam, whose patience and good humor have proven unflagging over two years of interaction, basically borders near sainthood, and we have been the happy beneficiaries of this paragon's enormous range of estimable virtues. Thanks also to Virginia Ruebens for an extraordinary copyediting job.

During this momentous year in our lives, we have been privileged to meet many wonderful booksellers who believed in our book and hand-sold it magnificently. We are grateful to all of you, too numerous to mention, and we applaud your efforts. There are two small independent stores, however, that deserve special mention. No store has championed *Small Miracles* more fervently than Harnik's Happy House in Brooklyn. Noreen Harnik and Terri Roca and their devoted staff threw such incredible support behind *Small Miracles* that they made it into the number one all-time best-selling book in their store's fifty-year history! We will be forever indebted to them for their tremendous generosity of heart and magnanimity of spirit. Edna Krausz of Inspiration Gallery in New Rochelle, New York, fell in love with

*Small Miracles* and sold it in a big way in her neck of the woods. To date, this store — small in size but very large in stature — has sold more than 600 copies of *Small Miracles*, all due to the very devoted hand-selling of the proprietor.

We are both members of an informal women's group, which stresses spirituality and creative living, and we want to thank the very special members of the group for their ongoing support and genuine sharing in our success. Thank you Pessie, Etta, Ruchama, Hadas, Miriam, and Shulamis! We look forward to many years together. Also, a special thanks to Ruth Wolfert for her wisdom and guidance. Anna Ashton deserves tremendous applause for her devotion and help.

Finally, we would like to thank our agents, Gareth Esersky and Carol Mann, for bringing us to Adams Media, and for their guidance and support.

I would like to thank my colleagues at EMUNAH for their gracious support always, and for being willing to overlook many conspicuous absences this past year as a result of both book-tour and book-writing commitments.

Many special people have shared their stories and thoughts about coincidences with me, but I have been most recently touched and moved by the special generosity of Rabbi Hanoch Teller. Rabbi Teller, an outstanding scholar and renowned storyteller, does not jealously guard the gems he has collected, but very generously and graciously shares them with all.

The greatest moments in life are those shared by friends and family. The enthusiasm and support demonstrated by my dear friends — Raizy Steg, Bella Friedman, Annette Grauman, Babshi Berkowitz, Sarah Laya Landau, and Hindy Rozenberg — are very precious to me. Special thanks also to Ginny Duffy and Marcella Weiner for holding my hand when I most needed it. When the going got tough, I got going to one of the above. My family — my mother, Claire Halberstam; my brother, Moishe Halberstam; and my sister, Miriam Halberstam — have supported my efforts faithfully, as have my in-laws, Leib and Sima Mandelbaum; Suri and Danny Dymshits; Chaim and Bayla Mandelbaum; and Yeruchem and Chaya Winkler. Bayla ran out and bought the first copy of *Small Miracles* sold in Brooklyn the very day it came out, and Chaya threw a little celebration in her home. Both gestures meant so much to me. My sister, Miriam, devotedly scouted for coincidence stories on my behalf. Several of the stories published in this book emanated from her dedicated efforts, and I cannot thank her enough.

My two children — Yossi and Eli — have been joyous participants in the whole wonderful, exciting process and very indulgent of my deficiencies as a mother throughout. They have graciously forgiven me my flaws and absences during this hectic period. Yossi made many expeditions to various bookstores and agents in Israel in an attempt to promote the book there, and his efforts succeeded. Foreign rights to the book have now been sold to that country, and I thank Yossi for his role in making that happen. (Israel now joins Italy, Greece, Latin America, Brazil, China, Japan, Indonesia, Spain, Germany, and Korea in buying foreign rights to *Small Miracles*.)

My husband, Motty, to whom I have dedicated this book, is actually responsible — more than anybody else — for nurturing my creativity during adulthood. (My father of blessed memory was the primary source during childhood.) Throughout the twenty-one years of our marriage, Motty has always insisted, sincerely and with genuine devotion, that I eschew the kitchen in favor of my desk, and he has always reveled in my successes. His wisdom and good counsel have helped me on dozens of occasions, and his feedback and input have proven pivotal. More than anything else, living with him and being exposed to his brilliant insights and original way of thinking has helped me grow.

*— Yitta Halberstam*


I thank Jules, my dear beloved husband who has continuously shown me how to face my perceived limitations, challenge them and move beyond. With an abundance of love, he has stood by me and cheered me on.

I want to acknowledge my little toddler, Arielle who escorted me on the book tour. On the planes and off the planes, she marched like a little trooper, with backpack, stuffed teddy bear, wheeling her little carriage all around town. She made the trips a joy with her ability to delight in it all.

Estee, my sister, friend, and confidant has been a blessing in my life since the moment she was born. My dear mother, Rose, and Hedy and Myer Feiler and children, Isser and Malku Handler, Anne Leventhal, Emery, David and Shulamit Leventhal and children have all provided a loving and supportive family.

Much gratitude is also extended to Pesi Dinnerstein who is my beacon of light. Sara Barris, Deena Edelman, Ruchama and Yisrael Feuerman, and Eta Ansel have been close friends who have been so generous with their enthusiasm. Elli Wohlgelernter is a dear friend and has loved coincidences all his life. And lastly, I want to acknowledge Jonathan and Ruchy Mark who have, through their words, reflected back to us the beauty of our book and together, they have been the catalyst for many miracles.

*— Judith Leventhal*

# Permissions

Grateful acknowledgment is made to the following for permission to reprint previously published material:

"Caught in a Firestorm" by Timothy S. Wright, February 1996. Reprinted by permission of *Guideposts Magazine*. Copyright ©1996 by Guideposts, Carmel, NY.

"The Hand of Dog" by Glen Martin, May 19, 1994. Reprinted by permission from *The San Francisco Chronicle*.

"Hands of Fate Reunite Women, Stolen Rolex" by Arnold Markowitz, May 7, 1997. Reprinted by permission from *The Miami Herald*.

"Lessons in Emunah" edited by Naomi Mauer. Reprinted by permission from *The Jewish Press*.

"I Can Do Anything" by Veronica Chater and Arlene Nunes, May 20, 1997. Reprinted with permission by *Woman's World Magazine*, Englewood Cliffs, New Jersey.

Excerpt from *Incredible Coincidence: The Baffling World of Sychronicity*. Copyright ©1979 by Alan Vaughn. Reprinted by permission of Harper Collins Publishers.

"My Life is Yours" by Jeff Smith, July 1996. Reprinted with permission from *Guideposts Magazine*. Copyright ©1996 by Guideposts, Carmel, NY.

Excerpt from *Not by the Sword* by Kathryn Watterson. Reprinted by permission of Ellen Levine Agency, Inc. Copyright ©1995 by Kathryn Watterson.

"Rollaway Plan" by Faye Field, February 1996. Reprinted with permission from *Guideposts Magazine*. Copyright ©1996 by Guideposts, Carmel, NY.

Excerpt from *Shining Lights* by Ruchoma Shain. Reprinted by permission from Feldheim Publishers, Nanuet, BY and Ruchoma Shain.

"Three Sisters Deliver Amazin' Triple Play" by Roger Field, February 1, 1997. Reprinted by permission from *The New York Post*.

# Small Miracles

A nationwide bestseller, *Small Miracles* is the original collection of sixty true life stories of remarkable coincidences that have changed the lives of ordinary people. Moving, heartwarming, and inspirational, the stories contain important moral lessons, profound teachings, and even divine messages.

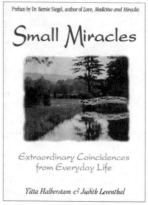

Preface by Dr. Bernie Siegel, author of *Love, Medicine and Miracles*

## Small Miracles

*Extraordinary Coincidences from Everyday Life*

*Yitta Halberstam & Judith Leventhal*

Trade paperback, $7.95, ISBN: 1-55850-646-2

## Available Wherever Books Are Sold

If you cannot find this title at your favorite retail outlet, you may order it directly from the publisher. BY PHONE: Call 1-800-872-5627 (in Massachusetts 781-767-8100). We accept Visa, Mastercard, and American Express. $4.50 will be added to your total order for shipping and handling. BY MAIL: Write out the full title of the book you'd like to order and send payment, including $4.50 for shipping and handling, to: Adams Media Corporation, 260 Center Street, Holbrook, MA 02343. 30-day money-back guarantee.

Send us your own small miracles: Have you ever experienced an unusual, heartwarming, or mysterious coincidence? We would like to hear about these personal events, and possibly use them for an upcoming sequel.

*Small Miracles*
Adams Media Corporation
260 Center Street
Holbrook, MA 02343

All submissions will become the property of Adams Media Corporation.